Blue Skies Travel Guide

Borneo

David Bowden

First published in the United Kingdom in 2018 by John Beaufoy Publishing Ltd
11 Blenheim Court, 316 Woodstock Road, Oxford OX2 7NS, England
www.johnbeaufoy.com

Photo Credits
All photographs taken by David Bowden except those listed on p. 158:

ISBN 978-1-912081-51-6

Edited by Krystyna Mayer
Indexed by Marie Lorimer
Designed by Gulmohur Press, New Delhi
Project management by Rosemary Wilkinson

Printed and bound in Malaysia by Times Offset (M) Sdn. Bhd.

CONTENTS

Note Many geographical features and place names have both Bahasa and English names. Both have been used, with the most common name listed. Note the following Bahasa names and their English meaning: *gunung* (mountain), *bukit* (hill), *taman* park, *pulau* (island), *kampong/kampung* (village), *sungai* (river), *pantai* (beach) and *kuala* (estuary).

PART 1: INTRODUCTION

Mount Kinabalu in Sabah is the highest peak in Borneo at 4,095m (13,435ft).

One of the world's largest islands, Borneo has unique flora and fauna, a broad cultural diversity and a frontier existence that now appeals to adventurous travellers. Those who venture to this remote part of the world soon discover that Borneo lives up to the legends, and reveals a lot more to those who take the time to absorb all that it has to offer.

Introduction to Borneo

The island of Borneo is on the itinerary of many travellers, and there are few islands in the world that evoke the sense of adventure, mystery, fascination and romance that Borneo does.

In the past, tales about the world's third largest island (after Greenland and New Guinea, excluding Australia, which is the largest island continent) filtered back to the known world, and adventurers, merchants and traders set out to make their fortunes. Inquisitive scientists followed as did missionaries, then came the loggers, miners and plantation companies.

Borneo covers an area of 743,330km² (287,000 sq miles) and is surrounded by the South China Sea (west), Sulu Sea (north-east), Celebes Sea and Makassar Strait (east), and Java Sea and Karimata Strait (south). Its highest peak is Mount (or Gunung) Kinabalu in Sabah, at 4,095m (13,435ft).

Proboscis Monkeys are commonly found in mangroves.

Green Cover

From the air, large tracts of Borneo have 'green' cover but this does not mean that they are primary forests; the World Wide Fund for Nature (WWF) suggests that more than half of them have been modified through human intervention. The biggest threats to the forests are land conversion, poor forest management, forest fires and illegal logging.

The existing primary rainforests are more than 130 million years old, yet they are one of the least understood ecosystems in the world. Scientists still unearth new species on a weekly basis, with some even suggesting that potential cures for diseases could be in these forests awaiting discovery.

The forests are home to many animals, some of which are endemic to Borneo. Scientists have identified 63 endemic mammals and 61 endemic birds (the possible inclusion of another eight bird species is still debated).

Coral Triangle

The late science-fiction writer and keen scuba diver Arthur C. Clarke noted how inappropriate it was to talk about Planet

Borneo's Top Ten Mammals
Bearded Pig
Bornean Orangutan
Clouded Leopard
Hose's Langur
North Borneo Gibbon
Proboscis Monkey
Pygmy Elephant
Red Langur
Sumatran Rhinoceros
Sun Bear

Borneo is part of the Coral Triangle.

Bornean Pygmy Elephant.

One of the most acclaimed naturalists to work in Borneo was British-born Alfred Russel Wallace. He independently conceived the theory of evolution through natural selection for which Charles Darwin, of *On the Origin of Species* fame, is best known. In 1854, Wallace met up with the first White Rajah, James Brooke who was in Singapore giving evidence to a special commission. Brooke offered Wallace every assistance in exploring the territories under his rule (Sarawak). Wallace made a decision to travel to Borneo rather than Cambodia and, in so doing, dramatically increased the body of scientific knowledge about the island. He spent 15 months in Borneo collecting scientific specimens and sending them back to England. In Sarawak, by the mouth of the Sarawak River immediately opposite present-day Bako National Park, he started conceptualising his theories on the origin of species. He later went to Bali and Lombock (Lombok) and noticed that there was a marked difference between the plants and animals on the two islands though they were quite close to each other geographically. In so doing, he discovered the dividing line between the Australian and Asian biological regions, which today is still known as the Wallace Line.

Lowland tropical rainforests once covered much of Borneo.

Earth when it was quite clearly mostly Ocean. Borneo's marine environments have major ecological and tourism importance.

Borneo is in the middle of what is known as the Coral Triangle, which extends from Sumatra eastwards to the Solomon Islands in the Pacific Ocean. Its waters harbour the largest collection of coral reefs in the world, and in turn the corals support vast numbers of other marine organisms. The Coral Triangle is home to some 600 species of coral, 3,000 fish species and the largest extent of mangrove forests anywhere on Earth. Some 75 per cent of all the world's coral reef species survive in the Coral Triangle as do six of the world's seven species of marine turtle. Known as the 'Amazon of the Oceans', the Coral Triangle is vitally important as the nursery of the sea for many species that are of benefit not only to science but also to humans as a source of food.

Over 120 million people are known to live in the Coral Triangle and rely upon the coral reefs for their livelihood, food and the protection from storms that the reefs provide.

WWF has documented concerns about unsustainable fishing practices and the harvesting of reef resources plus the threats climate change pose to these coastal communities living adjacent to coral reefs. Commercial fishing and over-fishing is also closely monitored by environmental groups and some governments.

The People

While many of the 20 million people in Borneo live sophisticated urban lives as people do in other parts of the world, visitors do not have to travel far from built-up areas to be in the 'wilds of Borneo'.

Just as the island's flora and flora are unique, so too are many of the tribes that live on the island. When the Dutch arrived they called all non-Malay inland tribes Dayaks, but there are numerous distinct differences within the Dayaks (these days the term Dayak is only used in Kalimantan). Many people recognize that at least 40 sub-ethnic groups of people live in Borneo, but WWF notes that there are 50 Dayak groups alone speaking different languages.

A number of communities choose to reside in communal longhouses (*rumah betang* in Indonesia and *rumah panjang* in Malaysia), and only a few tribes are considered nomadic hunter-gatherers. Some of the 10,000 known Penan people still live such a lifestyle, but even most of them now live sedentary lives in permanent settlements.

The people of Borneo include Apo Kayan/Orang Ulu, Ngaju, Murut, Bidayuh, Punan, Ot Danum, Malays (Melayu), Chinese, Iban, Bidayuh, Orang Ulu, Melanau, Murut, Kedayan, Orang Ulu, Kayan, Lun Bawang, Kenyah, Kelabit, Penan, Sebup, Bisaya, Kadazan-Dusun, Bajau, Murut, Indian, Eurasian, Javanese and Bugis, plus a myriad sub-ethnic groups.

While many tribespeople once wore colourful clothing, they mostly only do so these days for ceremonies or cultural performances at venues such at the Sarawak Cultural Village in Damai(see pp. 96–97). Tattoos, earlobe extension and brass rings around legs were once common with some communities in Borneo. Bidayuh women, for example, once used to cover their lower legs with brass rings; a practice that was unique amongst Bornean people. The first two are still practised by many young people and are popular with some travellers to Borneo.

Borneo has many different ethnic communities including the Iban.

Ten Essential Borneo Experiences

Borneo has many things to see, places to explore, cultures to experience and people to meet. Narrowing these experiences down to ten is difficult, but here are those that make travelling in the island so unique.

Wild Orangutans

Orangutans are only found on the islands of Borneo and Sumatra. There are several rehabilitation centres that make it easier to see them than is possible in the wild (see pp. 34–35). The centres have been established to rehabilitate orphaned Orangutans, or those rescued from captivity, for later release into the wild. Feeding sessions are the best times to view Orangutans in natural surroundings. Centres include Sepilok (Sabah), Semenggoh and Matang (Sarawak), and Ketapang, Gunung Palung and Tanjung Puting (Kalimantan).

Many travel to see Orangutans in the wild.

Trainspotting

Sabah State Railway operates Borneo's only passenger track, and for some villagers the train from Kota Kinabalu to Tenom provides the only way out of the Padas Valley. The suggested journey involves taking the 140-km (87-mile) trip to Tenom, spending the night and retracing the journey the next morning. The privately owned North Borneo Railway has twice-weekly tourist steam trains to Papar, 70km (44 miles) south of Kota Kinabalu.

Mountain Climbing

At 4,095m (13,435ft) Mount Kinabalu (see pp. 32–33) is Borneo's – and indeed the whole of Malaysia's – highest mountain, and making the two-day summit climb is a rite of passage for adventurers. Daily numbers are limited to 135 climbers, so bookings for fit climbers are essential.

Caving

Some of the world's largest caves extend below the forests and limestone peaks in the World Heritage Site of Gunung Mulu National Park in northern Sarawak (see pp. 38–39). Most visitors fly into the remote park to enjoy its excellent facilities.

Diving

Rated as one of the world's best dive sites, Sipadan and nearby Mabul and Kapalai

Islands (see pp. 84–85) are on most divers' wish lists. Malaysia's only oceanic island, Sipadan, rises 600m (2,000ft) from the bed of the Celebes Sea. Bookings are essential as diving permits are limited.

Forest Trekking

Lowland dipterocarp forest once covered Borneo, but agricultural development has resulted in forest clearing. Brunei's untouched Ulu Temburong forests are therefore important for biological diversity and research.

Fascinating Flora

A flower of *Rafflesia arnoldii* reaches a diameter of 100cm (39in), and the flowers of the other 27 *Rafflesia* species are also large. The parasitic flower takes months to develop but remains in full bloom for only a few days, making its observation difficult. These fascinating plants can be seen at the Rafflesia Information Centre in Tambunan, Sabah (see pp. 64–65).

Floating Market

Lok Baintan Floating Market (see p. 139) near Banjarmasin in South Kalimantan is different from Borneo's other fresh produce markets in that trading is done from boats on the Martapura River. The best time to visit is before sunrise, using the services of a guide and a *klotok* boat.

Longhouse Living

Many tribal communities live in longhouses, which consist of a single structure under one roof with a communal verandah and separate family quarters. Longhouses are common especially in the Sarawak interior, and are important not just for their architecture but also for the social structure of those living this communal lifestyle. Travel up the Rajang River or across Batang Ai (see pp. 100–103) to enjoy longhouse hospitality.

Mulu Caves are some of the world's biggest.

Saving Turtles

There are several places in which visitors can see turtles. In Turtle Islands National Park (see pp. 36–37) in the Sulu Sea off Sandakan, there is a turtle hatchery and accommodation for visitors. Turtles lay eggs nightly and the highlight is the release of hatchlings into the sea. There is also a turtle hatchery on Talang Island off Damai, and turtles are abundant in the waters surrounding Derawan Island in East Kalimantan.

About Borneo

The fact that Borneo is the world's third largest island should be sufficient for people to have an interest in and curiosity about this land that straddles the Equator, but perhaps it is what people do not know about Borneo that is as intriguing as what is known. For example, apart from the scores of new species discovered annually by scientists, Cambridge University researchers recently located the world's largest tropical tree, 94.1m (398ft) in height and growing ever higher skywards in Sabah's Danum Valley.

Geography

Many people have the impression that Borneo is covered in impenetrable rainforest that harbours dangerous animals and mysterious tribes of headhunters. While this may have once been closer to the truth than it is today, times have changed. In the deepest, remotest rainforests, some tribal communities still live a subsistence lifestyle, but their numbers are limited.

Borneo covers an area of 743,330km^2 (287,000 sq miles), comprising Kalimantan (73 per cent), Sarawak/Sabah (27 per cent) and Brunei (1 per cent). It is also an island surrounded by hundreds of other islands, ranging from mere specks on the horizon to substantive and settled islands such as Banggi (off the northern tip of Sabah) and the Federal Territory of Labuan (off the far western extent of Sabah). Other important tourist islands off the main island of Borneo include Turtle Islands and Lankayan Island (Sabah), the popular diving islands of Sipadan, Mabul and Kapalai off East Sabah, and the Derawan Group off East Kalimantan.

Borneo island's highest summit is Mount Kinabalu in Sabah, at 4,095m (13,435ft), while the highest peak in Sarawak is Mount Trusmadi (2,641m/8,665ft); in Central Kalimantan it is Bukit Raya (2,300m/7,546ft) and in Brunei, Bukit Pagon (1,850m/6,070ft).

Access to the interior of Borneo has always been difficult, and its rivers have been and still are important links for upriver communities to the outside world. Borneo's longest river is the Mahakam in

East Kalimantan, at 920km (570 miles) in length. In Sarawak, the longest river is the Rajang (565km/351 miles), in Sabah it is the Kinabatangan (560km/350 miles) and in Brunei the Belait (41km/25 miles).

It is not only the land features that make Borneo so fascinating, but also what is in the waters surrounding the island and in subterranean caves located beneath the forest cover.

Borneo is divided into three countries: Malaysia (the states of Sabah and Sarawak), Indonesia (Kalimantan) and Brunei Darussalem. Additionally, the small island of Labuan is a Malaysian federal territory. Its economy depends mainly on agriculture, timber, oil and gas and ecotourism. Brunei is one of the largest producers of oil in Southeast Asia. Sabah and Sarawak are top exporters of timber as well as liquefied natural gas and petroleum. Sabah's agricultural products are rubber, cacao and fish. Kalimantan is involved in mining plus oil and gas exploration.

River journeys are often the only way to access parts of Borneo.

History

Before the last Ice Age and the rising of the seas, Borneo, Java and Sumatra were connected to mainland Asia. However, Borneo was not connected to Sulawesi due to its deeper waters. This led to different flora developing in Asia and Australia-New Guinea, as identified by Wallace's Line (named after Alfred Russel Wallace, see p. 6, who first documented this division).

Indian, Japanese and Chinese merchants have traded with communities in Borneo for 1,000 years. They exploited forest products and minerals like gold, camphor, rhinoceros horn, hornbill casques, rattan and swiftlet nests, exchanging them for ceramics, earthenware containers and textiles. The Brunei Empire once covered the northern part of Borneo and southern Philippines. It, and the Sulu Empire (southern Philippines), declined with the arrival of Western powers.

European contact was first made in the 16th century, when the Portuguese, Dutch and British in that order started trading with coastal communities. Over time, mercantile enterprises like the Dutch East India Company and the British East India Company dominated trade here and in the neighbouring Spice Islands.

The British East India Company (EIC) was established at the beginning of the 17th century as a chartered syndicate of traders and operated under a loose royal monopoly. Like several other European companies, particularly in Holland and Portugal, it was the pursuit of spices that motivated these mercantile entrepreneurs.

Bill Bryson in his book *At Home* notes that 'a very big part of the history of the modern world is the history of spices'. He adds that 'spices were not just the world's most valued foodstuffs, they were the most treasured commodities of any type'. Pepper was the spice that first captured the attention of Europeans (still today, Sarawak pepper is considered a highly prized spice with gourmands). Commodities such as nutmeg (mace), cloves, cinnamon, ginger and turmeric followed.

Spices were a major factor in Borneo's history.

The expansion of the EIC was often left in the hands of those 'in the field' in the countries where it operated, like India and the Malaysian island of Penang. Over time, the needs of the government took precedence over those of the company as a series of measures saw the steady increase in central governmental control. The EIC was more active in Penang, Malacca (now Melaka) and Singapore than Borneo.

In what is now Indonesia, the Dutch East India Company (Verenigde Oost-Indische Compagnie or VOC) operated as a multinational corporation between 1602 and 1799. It, too, started as a chartered company to trade with the East. The Dutch government allowed it a monopoly in order to control spice prices and to manage the risks of trading these spices. The company came under the administration of the Dutch Government in 1800. The VOC issued bonds and shares to the public and thus became the world's first formally listed public company and possibly the first globalized company centuries before the word entered the vocabulary of trade.

Parts of Borneo (present day Kalimantan) remained independent, others as outposts of the VOC, as its business interests were focussed on the island of Java. The expansion of Dutch territory was very much a business matter with company profitability the official policy. This changed in 1840 and Dutch national expansion resulted in a series of wars and consolidation over their possessions in the outer islands. This was partly done to prevent other Western powers extending their power in the region.

The Dutch extended their influence in South Kalimantan during the Banjarmasin War (1859–1863), which saw the sultan defeated by the superior foreign force. It became a Dutch protectorate in 1891. The Dutch arrived peacefully in West Kalimantan in 1884 after the sultan sought their protection.

North Borneo was initially established by concessions of the Sultanates of Sulu and Brunei in 1877 to a German-born representative of Austria-Hungary. Gustav Oberbeck (later Baron) was an adventurer, businessman and diplomat who moved to the United States as a young man before undertaking trade trips to Hawaii, Alaska and the Bering Strait.

He came into contact with the English trading house Dent & Co who were English merchants active in China in the 19th century. British brothers Alfred and Edward Dent operated the North Borneo Chartered Company from 1881 to 1946.

Even the Americans were interested, and they established the American Trading Company of Borneo in Kimanis, south of Kota Kinabalu. Kimanis is now a stop on the Tenom train (see pp. 54–55).

Oberbeck joined Dent & Co in 1854 in British Hong Kong and became a consul to the Chinese Empire in 1864. In 1876, he purchased the concessionary rights of the American Trading Company of Borneo.

In 1881, Oberbeck transferred his rights to the Dent Brothers and the British North Borneo Provisional Association Limited. This pushed back the claim of the territory by the Sultan of Sulu and the Spanish who were then influential in what is now known as the Philippines. This transfer of 'ownership' is still central to the territorial dispute over Sabah between Malaysia and the Philippines.

Unknown grave, Labuan.

White Rajah Charles Brooke Memorial in Kuching.

In 1888 North Borneo became a protectorate of Great Britain but control effectively remained in the hands of the company until 1942 when the Japanese invaded and took control over all of Borneo. The Japanese occupation lasted until they signed an unconditional surrender in Labuan on 15 September 1945.

While various sultans continued ruling, many surrendered their powers to the more powerful Europeans. For example, in present-day Sarawak, the Sultan of Brunei ceded land to English adventurer James Brooke in return for resolving a conflict between warring tribes. Brooke and his descendants ruled Sarawak as the White Rajahs from 1841 to 1946.

History suggests that James Brooke was in the right place at the right time. He sailed from Singapore to Borneo with a message from the then governor of Singapore to be delivered to the Raja Muda (Sultan) of Brunei. He arrived to help quell a riot among the local Iban community who resented the treatment they received from the sultan.

Piracy in the region was also rife and the Chinese traders living in Sarawak suffered. After supressing the disgruntled locals, Brooke launched several successful anti-piracy campaigns. In 1841, the sultan offered him governorship over Sarawak and in 1842; the sultan ceded complete sovereignty of Sarawak to Brooke. Brooke was also given the title of Rajah.

James Brooke (later Sir James Brooke) was the absolute ruler of Sarawak until 1868. Brooke never married and he was succeeded by his nephew Charles Brooke who ruled until 1918. Then, his son Vyner ruled until 1946 although the Japanese occupied Sarawak during the Second World War. After the war, the rule of the White Rajahs came to an end when they ceded the state to the United Kingdom.

While their rule was absolute, they were determined to prevent the indigenous peoples of Sarawak from being exploited by Western business interests. Their rule is generally considered to have been favourable to the state and its peoples.

The Second World War was an important time in Borneo. The lives of many locals were disrupted, and Borneo housed thousands of Allied prisoners of war, most of whom were British and Australian, captured when Singapore fell.

Two camps were established, in Sandakan and Batu Lintang (Kuching). Conditions were harsh, with prisoners being mistreated and becoming malnourished. Thousands of Javanese

Memorial chapel for the Sandakan Death March victims.

forced labourers also perished, as did locals who assisted the Allies. Resistance groups aided by Allied Z Special Forces staged guerrilla warfare against the Japanese.

After the Second World War, nations demanded independence from their colonial masters. Indonesia was first in 1945, Sarawak and Sabah joined the Malaysian Federation in 1957, and Brunei Darussalam became an independent nation in 1984.

Under the terms and conditions of Sarawak and Sabah joining the Federation was the right of each state to a degree of state-level control over their borders. This means that today, both maintain their own customs and immigration procedures in addition to those operated in the rest of the country. Despite having already been through immigration procedures in West Malaysia, visitors to Sarawak and Sabah will have their passport re-checked and re-stamped when entering each of the states. Even Malaysians from West Malaysia have to show their national identification cards to enter either East Malaysian state and they are not allowed to work there unless they have already obtained a special permit.

Security remains an issue in parts of Borneo especially some areas in the eastern parts of Sabah. Terrorist and separatist activity in neighbouring southern Philippines occasionally spills over into Sabah. In early 2013, an armed group of fighters from southern Philippines calling themselves the Royal Sulu Army intruded into Sabah in an effort to reclaim it for the defunct Sultanate of Sulu. Several dozen intruders were killed along with some Malaysian security forces and civilians.

Sandakan Death March

Some of the Second World War's darkest incidents were the Sandakan Death Marches, when Allied prisoners of war were forced to march across 250 km (155 miles) of mountainous jungle from Sandakan camp to Ranau near Mount Kinabalu. Documented in Lynette Ramsay Silver's *Sandakan A Conspiracy of Silence*, the three marches involved more than 1,000 Australian and British prisoners remaining from the 2,434 originally incarcerated in the camp. In response to orders from the Japanese High Command that no prisoner was to survive the war, the prisoners were marched across Borneo with about 75 per cent on the first march reaching the destination. The conditions along the way or at the destination camps killed them – they either died or were 'disposed of'. Of the three marches, just six survived to tell the tale of horrific maltreatment, starvation, beatings and murder. There is a memorial at the former camp and various plaques around Borneo to remind visitors of the Second World War. The Labuan Commonwealth World War II cemetery contains the remains of 3,908 prisoners.

The People

Borneo is home to 20 million people, although the remotest communities are unlikely to be included in this total. Numerous people now live an urban existence, and while international cultural performances are staged in places such the Sarawak Cultural Village in Damai (see pp. 96–97), many communities maintain their cultural traditions locally and are happy to share them with visitors.

There are more than 40 ethnic tribes or communities living in Borneo, with the bulk of these being known in Kalimantan as Dayaks. The Ibans are a branch of the Dayaks and mostly live in Sarawak. They were formerly known during colonial times as Sea Dayaks, and were renowned and feared for practising headhunting and piracy.

Traditionally animist, many Ibans are now Christians, but some communities continue to observe both Christian and traditional ceremonies, particularly during marriages and festivals. While some communities still live a longhouse existence, most are equipped with electricity, water, telephones and the Internet.

Culture, Music and Dance

Festivals are important to most tribes in Borneo, with the end of the harvest being significant for many. Dance, song and music are performed to accompany special dishes and, in some communities, the consumption of rice wine, or *tuak*.

The Iban as well as the Kayan also play an instrument resembling the lute, called a *sape*, and their music is widely identified as the music of Sarawak (exponents appear annually at Sarawak's Rainforest World Music Festival). Nose flutes are played in some communities, such as the Kenyan, Penan and Rungus. They were traditionally played by males and females during courtship, or at funerals to appease the spirits of the recently deceased.

Longhouses have a communal verandah area for the community to socialise.

Ibans perform a dance called the *ngajat*, which serves many purposes depending upon the occasion. During Gawai (the end of the harvest festival), women perform this graceful dance. *Ngajat* for men is more aggressive and depicts someone going off to battle, or as a mimic of a hornbill bird.

It is not unusual to see older women weaving *pua kumbu*, the traditional Iban cotton cloth blanket, made using traditionally dyed thread (*ikat*) and woven on a back-strap loom. These. looms are often used by women, who work sitting on the floor of communal areas of a longhouse. Animals and plants are commonly portrayed in the designs; natural dyes were once used but commercial ones are now more common.

Borneo also has a strong tradition of creating beadwork, with glass and stone being used originally, although other materials are utilized in the more commercial designs now sold in souvenir shops all over Borneo. Teeth, bones and shells were also incorporated into beadwork, which was used as ornamentation and as a status symbol. Beadwork was and still is used to decorate utilitarian items such as baby carriers, jewellery boxes and baskets.

Basketry is another important craft in Borneo. Baskets originally served purely functional purposes, such as carrying and storing goods in communities like the Lun Bawang. Rigid (using supplementary wood) or soft baskets are made, but these days natural products from the forest such as rattan, bamboo, pandanus, reeds and grasses have mostly been replaced by artificial materials like plastic. Basketwork is employed in the making of mats, bags, hats and baby carriers. These are traditionally produced by women, with mothers passing

Borneo has a long tradition of beadworking.

their skills on to their daughters.

While the women of Borneo weaved, the men carved wood, which was important not only for its utilitarian purposes in construction, but also for use in making coffins, grave posts, spirit ladders, rice *padi* gods, masks, bird cages, doors and hornbill carvings. White kaolin was often used to decorate the timber, along with other materials sourced from nature.

Body adornments such as tattoos and elongated ear lobes play important roles in some tribal groups. Jewellery, especially with floral motifs, has been used for centuries. Brass coins (Dutch and British) and wooden discs are also commonly used in earrings, silver headdresses and armlets.

Biodiversity

Biodiversity is the sum total of living organisms (including humans) in marine, terrestrial and aquatic ecosystems. Scientists refer to species richness as a measure of the complexity and ecological importance of an ecosystem, and the rainforests and waters surrounding Borneo are some of the richest and most important of any ecosystem in the world.

Scientists have recorded in Borneo 15,000 plants , of which 2,500 are orchid species and 50 carnivorous pitcher plants, 1,400 bird, mammal, fish, amphibian and reptile species, plus an unknown number of insects. Of Borneo's 222 recorded mammal species, 44 are endemic (found nowhere else in the world) and of the 15,000 plants, some 6,000 are considered to exist only in Borneo. This provides ecotourists with even more reasons for visiting the island.

One of the fascinating facts about the rainforests of Borneo is the high plant speciation. In his book *A Short History of Almost Everything* celebrated author Bill Bryson makes reference to Edward O. Wilson's book *The Diversity of Life* and notes that the botanist spent a few days tramping around 10ha (25 acres) of jungle in Borneo and discovered a thousand new species of flowering plant, more than all found in the whole of the North American continent. Bryson comments that: "the plants weren't hard to find, it's just that no one looked there before." He adds: "Overall, tropical rainforests cover only 6 per cent of Earth's surface, but they harbour more than half of its animal life and about two-thirds of its flowering plants – and most of this life remains unknown to us because too few researchers spend time in them."

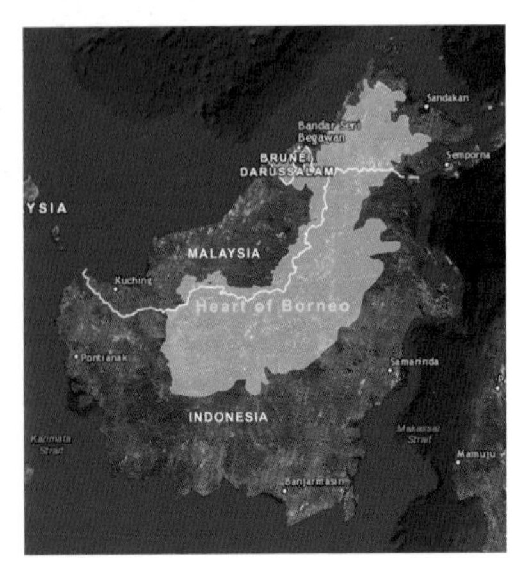

The Heart of Borneo refers to the main part of the island where forests remain intact.

WWF notes that while Borneo occupies just 1 per cent of the world's total land mass, it supports 6 per cent of all known biodiversity.

As a start, the governments of Indonesia, Malaysia and Brunei have agreed to protect 220,000km^2 (85,000 sq miles) of forests in Borneo under the Heart of Borneo project. These transboundary forests comprise 30 per cent of the island, extending over national boundaries in mostly remote parts of the Borneo interior.

Heart of Borneo was established in 2010 to protect the ecological and cultural richness of rainforests by putting in place sustainable management practices. People are very much at the heart of the project, with an estimated half a million indigenous people dependent on what is the largest expanse of rainforest in Southeast Asia. The Heart of Borneo Foundation works to assist the project, and interested travellers can join an expedition, conduct research or volunteer to assist.

Primary forest cover in Borneo is now estimated to be just 50 per cent, down

Crocodiles inhabit estuarine parts of Borneo.

substantially from historic records, with clearing of land for agriculture, plantations, logging and settlement taking its toll on the primary vegetation. Flora and fauna thrive in the variety of ecosystems in Borneo with the warm temperatures and abundant rainfall providing ideal conditions for life.

Ecotourism is important to the survival of the forests as it gives ongoing value to these natural areas that, in many cases, are seen as a resource to exploit. Ecotourism assigns sustainable value to the natural resources and provides communities with an income, while preserving these valuable resources.

Examples of Borneo's Unique Biodiversity

Flora

Rafflesia (world's largest flower)

Pitcher Plants (carnivorous)

Kerangas (heath forest)

Paphiopedilum rothschildianum (slipper orchid endemic to Kinabalu Park)

Arundina (bamboo orchids)

Podochilus (world's smallest orchids).

Eco-tours along rivers are often the best way to see wildlife.

The Natural Environment

Much of Borneo was once covered in primary vegetation such as lowland rainforest, montane forests in the higher altitudes and mangroves around the coasts. While development has altered some places, many natural areas still remain and some of these are reasonably accessible, if often only via long overland or river journeys.

The forests are important for global biodiversity, and scientists are calling for more sustainable development rather than the continued establishment of monocultures such as plantations, which are all too evident in Borneo today.

Scientists admit that they do not really know what there is yet to be discovered in Borneo's remotest parts – perhaps a cure for cancer or a solution for an energy-hungry world. WWF reports that 361 new species were identified in Borneo over the past decade. Some of these are small but others are quite large – among birds, for example,

Palm trees commonly grow in lowland tropical forests.

What Writers Say About Borneo

There are many historical accounts of journeys into the heart of Borneo. William T. Homaday observes in *The Experiences of a Hunter and Naturalist in the Malay Peninsula and Borneo* (1885): 'Nothing could be more arduous and full of risk of life and limb than overland travel in the interior of Borneo, where the traveller is confronted by dense, dark forests and rugged mountains from the beginning to the end of the journey. The interior is practically an uninhabited wilderness.'

Celebrated British novelist Somerset Maugham visited Borneo in the 1920s, and in his book *Borneo Stories* he details the account of a naturalist lost in the jungle. 'The undergrowth was so thick I couldn't see six feet into it and presently, I don't know if it was nerves or not, I had the sensation that some animal was walking stealthily behind me.'

Luxuriant plant growth occurs where the light can penetrate to lower levels of the forest.

the Spectacled Flowerpecker was not noticed and identified until 2009. Endemic to Borneo, it became the first new bird species to be identified in more than 100 years and surprisingly it was first seen in Danum Valley, where extensive scientific research has been ongoing since 1986. The bird is, however, a specialist canopy feeder, and because of this had eluded the watchful eyes of scientists and birdwatchers.

Worthy of note here is that a new Orangutan species was identified as recently as 2017 in the remote jungle of neighbouring Sumatra. With just 800 individual apes remaining, this new species, named the Tapanuli Orangutan (*Pongo tapanuliensis*), also officially became the world's most endangered great ape. In 1997, researchers at the Australian National University discovered an isolated population of Orangutans in Batang Toru south of the known habitat for Sumatran Orangutans. Since then, studies of their appearance, skulls, teeth and DNA have revealed a different species, but with common ancestry to the other two species. It is thought that the animals began to diverge into different species approximately 3.4 million years ago, and that the new species became isolated from its nearest relatives in Sumatra about 10,000–20,000 years ago.

Conservationists are concerned that the population of Orangutans in Borneo is rapidly declining especially in areas cleared for palm oil and acacia plantations, killed by hunters and by farm workers who shoot animals that encroach on agricultural land.

Key Endemic Species

Endemic species are plants or animals only found in one specific geographical location or region. In the case of Borneo there are some species that are found only on the island, or only in one part of it. For example, Kinabalu Park has four pitcher plant species that are found nowhere else in the world. Five rhododendrons are also endemic to the park, and the Kinabalu Friendly Warbler bird is found only in the park, and on Mount Trus Mardi just south of it.

Ornithologists have become fascinated by the possible naming of the Kinabalu Honey-buzzard, a rare black morph of the resident race of the Oriental Honey-buzzard, as a separate species. Further research may place eight other birds on the endemic bird list of Borneo, which currently includes 61 species. The possible contenders are the Cinereous Bulbul, Collared Owlet, Dark Blue Flycatcher, Hair-crested Drongo, Mountain Leaf-warbler, Purple-throated Sunbird, Rajah's Scops Owl and Spectacled Flowerpecker.

Maratua and Kakaban, the two largest of the Derawan Islands off East Kalimantan, are of interest to birdwatchers because two separate and endemic species are found on these islands. These are the Maratua Shama and Maratua Bulbul, along with endemic races of the Black-naped Blue Monarch, Hair-crested Drongo, Glossy Starling, Philippine Megapode, Blue-naped Parrot, and Purple-throated and Brown-throated Sunbirds.

The two islands of Maratua and Kakaban provide good examples of how endemism occurs. Along with the Malaysian islands of Layang Layang and Sipadan, they are the only four islands surrounding Borneo that were never connected to the mainland. Due to this, their ecology has developed in isolation from other communities of the mainland – hence their specific and unique bird species.

Brown-throated Sunbird

Cinereous Bulbul

Birds
There are currently 61 known endemic birds of Borneo including:
Bulwer's Pheasant
Bornean Barbet
Blue-headed Pitta
Dulit Partridge
Whitehead's Trogon
Mountain Barbet
Bristlehead
Pale-faced Bulbul
Mountain Wren Babbler
Friendly Bush Warbler

Scientific discoveries in recent years are quite staggering and indicate just how much is unknown about the island. Of the 105 lizards found in Borneo, 66 per cent survive in Gunung Mulu National Park (see pp. 38–39), and the recently discovered Mulu Flying Frog is endemic to the park.

Scientists have also discovered 51 new orchid species since 2007. Of the 5,000 flowering plants in Borneo, 34 per cent are endemic (a figure that is much higher than that of neighbouring Sumatra, which only has 12 per cent plant endemism).

While Borneo is very important at a micro level, it is for the large flora and fauna that most visitors travel to the island. The large mammals attract most of the attention, with the Bornean Orangutan near the top of every visitor's list. With 63 mammals being endemic to Borneo, there are at least 63 good reasons for visiting Borneo to try to see them in their natural environment.

Orangutan feeding in fruit tree.

Flora

Borneo is regarded as one of the world's hotspots for plant biodiversity, with Kinabalu Park being of specific ecological value. A biodiversity hotspot is an area that supports at least 1,500 plant species found nowhere else in the world, and which has at least 70 per cent of its original habitat intact.

Borneo is part of the Sundaland biodiversity hotspot, along with the neighbouring islands of Sumatra and Java. There is some concern among conservationists that Sundaland is being threatened by habitat destruction, with the 70 per cent limit being challenged by the pressures of development.

Some botanists think that Borneo may have the greatest plant diversity of any

The rafflesia is the world's largest flower but only stays in full bloom for a few days.

region on Earth. The amazing plants found here include the world's largest flower, which grows on plants of the *Rafflesia* genus. This parasitic plant is an icon of the plant kingdom. It develops on a host liana, but without any leaves, stems or roots, and it can take 16 months for it to grow from bud to flower. The flower only stays in full bloom for a few days, so to see it forest visitors need to be alert or seek the assistance of a forest guide who is aware of developments within the forest. Often the smell of the flower captures attention before it is sighted – it has an aroma resembling rotting flesh. Flies pollinate the male and female forms of the flower. *Rafflesia arnoldii* is the largest species of all the rafflesias. Two of the best places to see a rafflesia in full bloom are near Poring Hot Springs (see pp. 32–33) and the Rafflesia Information Centre in Tambunan, Sabah (see pp. 64–65).

Other amazing plants that thrive in parts of Borneo are the carnivorous *Nepenthes*, or pitcher plants. These have adapted to the lack of nutrients found in heath forests and some high-altitude montane forests. Rather than sourcing nutrients from the soil via a root system, pitcher plants have evolved with highly modified leaves in the shape of a pitcher or small container. A slimy liquid at the base of the container lures insects to it – once they make contact with the liquid the insects' fate is sealed and they cannot escape. A lip at the top and even a lid prevents any insects that do escape the liquid from crawling out. Insects are broken down by the liquid to provide nutrients to the plant.

The largest pitcher plant, *Nepenthes rajah*, can have a cup capacity of up to 2.5 litres (4.3 pints) – three times the size of a bottle of wine. Each species has a restrictive altitudinal occurrence and extremely limited distribution, and perhaps the most fascinating pitcher plants are those found at high altitudes in montane forests. Of the 31 *Nepenthes* species identified in Borneo, ten survive in Kinabalu Park (see pp. 32–33) and can most easily be identified on the summit trail up to a height of 3,300m (10,826ft).

Carnivorous pitcher plants are also known as 'monkey cups' as monkeys have been seen drinking from them.

Another adaptive quality for some heath forest plants is that they contain high levels of tannins and other toxins that make them unpalatable to browsing herbivores.

Fauna

Wildlife spotting in the rainforests of Borneo is never easy and patience is required. Many animals are camouflaged, flighty and nocturnal, but the good-natured guides available are well versed in the skills required to locate them.

For every large mammal and reptile seen, there are hundreds of insects, beetles, ants, spiders, frogs, butterflies and moths, so it is often best to concentrate on the macro level when looking out for wildlife. It is also a good idea to listen for the multitude of sounds emitted by frogs, and by insects such as cicadas. Scientists suggest that just one large lowland forest dipterocarp tree may support 1,000 insects.

Birds

Many of Borneo's endemic birds are montane species that have effectively become isolated on high land 'islands'. The Bornean Stubtail, Mountain Wren-warbler and Whitehead's Spiderhunter are examples.

The magnificent hornbills provide ornithological interest as they epitomize Borneo and are important to various tribal communities. The Rhinoceros Hornbill is not only the largest species, but also the emblem of Central Kalimantan and Sarawak. There are another seven species of hornbill in Borneo, including Pied Oriental and Wreathed Hornbills (see p. 82).

Riverbanks, wetlands and rice fields are excellent habitats for viewing waterbirds and raptors such as the White-bellied

Wreathed Hornbills prefer hill forest habitats.

Sea-eagle, Brahminy Kite, Cattle and Little Egrets, and Little Heron.

Mammals

Borneo has 247 mammal species (100 of them bats), 63 of which are endemic. Some are notoriously difficult to observe, so it is generally best to travel to Borneo with the view that seeing mammals in the wild is a bonus. However, the chances of seeing mammals are improved in rehabilitation areas like those established for Orangutans and Sun Bears.

Some animals, such as monkeys and pigs, which are not disturbed by humans, frequent areas of high human visitation such as the Visitor's Centre in Bako National Park (see pp. 40–41).

The best places to see primates such as the Proboscis Monkey, Long-tailed Macaque and Silvered Langur (also called the Silver Leafed Monkey or Silver Leaf Monkey) are along rivers where the animals freely leap between branches. The smallest of the primates is the Western Tarsier – being nocturnal it has huge eyes for its relatively small body.

The Bornean Pygmy Elephant is a subspecies of the Asian elephant. It is the smallest of all the species and mostly found in Sabah.

Bearded Pigs or signs of them (overturned soil and undergrowth) are common, especially on the edges of clearings or open spaces where they forage for roots and tubers by digging up the soil surface.

Reptiles and Amphibians

Perhaps the most commonly seen reptiles are Monitor Lizards, which grow to up to 2.5m (8ft). Loud movement in the undergrowth or a leafy area could be the first indication of the presence of a Malay Water Monitor lizard. This largest of Borneo's lizards is also a good swimmer, and while it looks like a long-distance runner it can become a sprinter in a matter of seconds.

Water Monitors are large ranging in size from 40cm (16in) to 1.5m (4ft 9in).

Gunung Mulu National Park (p. 38) is one of the best places to see amphibians as two thirds of all known Bornean species are found in the park.

Habitats

In its 'Borneo: Treasure Island at Risk' report, WWF outlined the environmental destruction that is occurring on the island due to agricultural expansion, illegal logging and poaching. Secondary forest replaces primary forest once it is cleared, although plantations now occupy vast tracts of former forests in many parts of Borneo.

Dipterocarp Forest

Many forests of Borneo are dominated by one family of trees, the dipterocarps. Hill dipterocarp forest commonly transitions to lowland dipterocarp forest at 900m (3,000ft) altitude, where oaks, laurels and myrtles appear. These are the most diverse and yet the most threatened of all Borneo forest habitats, with more than half of the primary forests having been cleared (WWF reports that 68 per cent of Kalimantan lowlands have been cleared, with the figure being 56 per cent for Malaysia).

Freshwater Swamp Forest

Two varieties of these forests exist – one develops on alluvial soils (riverine forest) and the other on infertile acidic soils (peat-swamp forest). Peat-swamp forests are Borneo's dominant form of lowland forest, and they develop where dead vegetation becomes waterlogged and is unable to decompose. Over the centuries layers of carbon dioxide-rich peat forms, but when the water is drained and the peat dries, it is susceptible to fire. Once alight, fires can smoulder for months and are difficult to extinguish.

Montane Forest

In Borneo this forest type generally occurs above 1,200m (4,000ft) in altitude. Tree heights in montane forests are lower and canopies less dense than in lowland forests, and estimates suggest that 70 per cent of the total of these forests is still intact. This may be because the timber is less favourable than that of lowland species

Mangrove forests grow best in saline and brackish conditions.

Nipa palm forest along the Kinabatangan River, Sabah.

(not as tall), and because the trees grow in steeper and more inaccessible locations.

Heath Forest (*Kerangas*)

These forests occur on well-drained sandy soils that are acidic and nutrient deficient. They tend to be lower in height than other forests and have a more simplistic biodiversity. Vegetation that can produce its own nutrients, like pitcher plants, thrives in this environment. One of the most accessible heath forests is located in Sarawak's Bako National Park (see pp. 40–41).

Mangrove and Nipa Forest

Mangroves are commonly found in coastal areas and estuaries as a boundary zone between the marine and terrestrial environments. WWF estimates that probably only 1.2 million hectares (2.9 million acres) or 20 per cent of original mangroves remain. The remainder was cleared for logging, aquaculture and agricultural extension. When sustainably logged, mangroves can provide valuable timber for charcoal production and general construction purposes. Nipa palms extend from the coasts and along tidal waters inland. The leaves have various uses from thatching to basketry.

Marine Habitats

Habitats on the land really only form half of Borneo's ecological story, with marine habitats having equal importance. Borneo is situated in the centre of the Coral Triangle, one of the world's greatest biodiversity hotspots. Coral reefs are the most species rich of all marine habitats, and while they only occupy 1 per cent of the oceans, they are home to 25 per cent of all fish species. These spawning grounds for fish are also economically important for the people of Borneo and the region.

Enjoying the Natural World

By their very nature, many natural areas in Borneo are wild places. They are the big attraction to visitors, even though the infrastructure in some of these places is limited, especially in wilderness areas like the Danum Valley and remote parks in Kalimantan.

Perhaps it is inaccessibility and limited infrastructure that ensure some parts of Borneo remain undeveloped. These hard-to-access destinations appeal to adventurers, although 'armchair adventurers' are also well catered for: accessible natural places near built-up areas are popular with those who want to see native animals in semi-natural surroundings.

Many animals are nocturnal and a night safari like the one offered in Sabah's Danum Valley provides a whole new perspective on the forest. Memorable experiences include walking along forest trails at night after the rain without a torch and seeing the bioluminescence on the forest floor.

Around 9 per cent of Kalimantan, 8 per cent of Sarawak and 14 per cent of Sabah is protected as some form of nature reserve. There are wonderful opportunities

Key Natural Places

Sabah
Danum Valley Conservation Area
Kinabalu Park
Kota Kinabalu Wetland Centre
Lower Kinabatangan River
Sepilok Forest Reserve
Tabin Wildlife Reserve
Tunku Abdul Rahman Park
Turtle Islands Parks

Sarawak
Bako National Park
Gunung Mulu National Park
Lambir Hills National Park
Lanjak Entimau Wildlife Sanctuary
Semenggoh Nature Reserve

Brunei
Brunei Bay
Labi Forest Reserve
Sungai Liang Forest Recreation Park
Ulu Temburong National Park

Kalimantan
Danau Sentarum
Derawan Archipelago
Gunung Palung
Gunung Raya
Kayan Mentarang National Park
Kutai National Park
Samboja Lestari Wildlife Reserve
Sungai Wain
Tanjung Puting

The elevated walkway at Sepilok's Rainforest Discovery Centre offers a unique rainforest insight.

Visitors to Mulu can see rainforest features on their way to visit the famous caves.

for wildlife sightings across Borneo, from remote wilderness areas to accessible Orangutan rehabilitation centres close to urban areas. This chapter highlights some key outstanding areas of wildlife interest.

Brunei's forests are considered some of the best preserved in the whole of Asia with 60 per cent untouched.

Tips for Wildlife Spotting

- Note that sighting wildlife in the rainforest is difficult.
- Be quiet and patient (seek out a hide if possible).
- Bear in mind that dawn and dusk are often the best times to spot wildlife.
- Use binoculars.
- Use the services of a local guide.
- Stay hydrated and use sunscreen.
- Read useful guides like *125 Best Birdwatching Sites in Southeast Asia, Phillipps' Field Guide to the Birds of Borneo, A Naturalist's Guide to the Birds of Malaysia, A Naturalist's Guide to the Birds of Borneo, Phillipps' Field Guide to the Mammals of Borneo, A Naturalist's Guide to the Butterflies of Borneo* and *A Naturalist's Guide to the Snakes of Southeast Asia.*

Cede Prudente's Wildlife-spotting Tips

Cede Prudente, who has provided the following tips, is a professional photographer and conservationist based in Sandakan, Sabah. He lives in one of the world's most diverse and exciting environments for wildlife photography. Cede operates North Borneo Safari, which offers a range of nature tourism adventures and conducts photo-safari and wildlife-watching trips to parks and wildlife reserves in Sabah. He can be contacted at www.cedeprudente.com.

1. Research the wildlife likely to be present at places being visited and learn about its behaviour and habitats.
2. Approach wildlife slowly and watch its behaviour closely; back off should animals look uncomfortable in your presence.
3. Handhold heavy telephoto lenses to anticipate and observe the flight path of a bird or the moving paths of other animals, and only lift a lense at the right moment.
4. The narrow field of view of super-telephoto lenses enables the photographer to isolate wildlife and creates surreal backgrounds. Move around to get the right background.
5. Get up early and rest at midday; be on the move again at dusk. Nocturnal animals are active from dusk to midnight, but avoid using a flash.

Kinabalu Park

At 4,095m (13,435ft), Mount Kinabalu, Malaysia's highest peak is also a hotspot of biodiversity, with some 6,000 plant species identified within the 753km^2 (291 sq mile) national park and UNESCO World Heritage Site,which it dominates.

While the mountain is sacred for the local Dusun people, the first recorded ascent in 1851 is attributed to Sir Hugh Low, who – through the plants he collected – alerted the scientific community to the mountain's unique flora.

Established in 1964, the park attracts global visitors, and while the challenge of a two-day climb to the summit at Low's Peak draws adventurous travellers, the cool air and biodiversity also appeal to those content to relax around the park headquarters.

The climb along the main route (Ranau Trail) normally takes two days with an overnight stop in comfortable accommodation halfway at Panalaban. An earthquake in 2015 killed 18 climbers and damaged the path. The main trail has been rerouted, the Mesilau Trail was closed and a new Kota Belud Trail is planned.

Mount Kinabalu is a giant volcanic dome comprising granite rock that is exposed at the summit. Vegetation changes with altitude from lowland dipterocarp to montane and subalpine forests. Conifers, oaks, rhododendrons, orchids, epiphytes and pitcher plants are found in higher altitudes.

Although the climb is not difficult it does involve a continuous ascent, while the return down many steps is jolting on the knees. For most people it is not a race, so constant resting is important – the length of the walk from the start at Timpohon Gate to the overnight rest is just 5km (3 miles). Climbers head off in the darkness of the second morning to reach the summit for the sunrise, then walk all the way down on the second day. However, the annual mountain climbathon sees athletes cover the return climb in two and a half hours.

*Atlas Moths (*Attacus atlas*) found in Borneo are considered the world's largest moths.*

All groups require a guide, foreigners pay substantially more than locals, porter services are optional and climbers should have warm clothing as temperatures at the summit are substantially lower than in the lowlands.

Mount Kinabalu is the home of Asia's first and the world's highest Via Ferrata (an iron cable fixed to the mountainside as an aid to climbers), at 3,766m (12,356ft).

Kinabalu Park is located 80km (50 miles) from Kota Kinabalu and is accessible by public buses that pass the park entrance. Visitors can stay in a variety of park accommodation or in the surrounding district of Ranau (see pp. 64–65). Restaurants, an interpretation centre and a souvenir shop complete the park's comprehensive facilities.

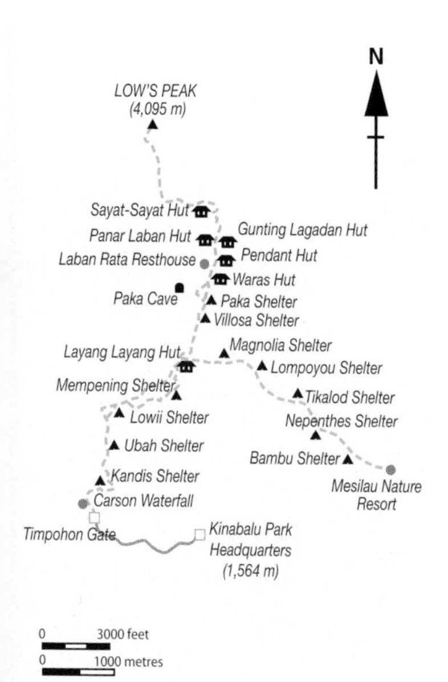

Map of the walking routes up Mount Kinabalu.

Wildlife Facts and Figures

Kinabalu is home to:
2 endemic shrews
10 pitcher plants
50 endemic ferns
100 mammals
326 birds
600 butterflies
750 orchids
1,000 moths
6,000 plants

Best Time to Visit

During the dry season from February to April.

Poring Hot Springs

Located an hour's drive from the park headquarters, Poring Hot Springs (see pp. 64–65) provides another entry point to the park. Natural hot spring water and pools are the main attraction, although the site also includes a canopy boardwalk, butterfly farm, tropical garden, orchid conservation centre, rafflesia flower site and accommodation.

Mount Kinabalu's peak is often shrouded in clouds.

Orangutans

As Orangutans only survive in the wilds of Borneo and Sumatra, these primates are one of the main animals visitors want to see in Borneo. Wild Orangutans are tree-dwelling primates that inhabit rainforests below 1,000m (3,281ft). Males live a solitary life, meeting with a female purely to mate, while females remain with their young until they are six years old. Their lifespan is 30 years and their diet consists of fruits, leaves, bark, flowers and insects.

Orangutans can be seen either in the wild or in the semi-natural surroundings of rehabilitation centres. There is debate on the need for captive and semi-captive Orangutan programmes, which are very popular with visitors. The oldest centre at Sepilok was established in Sabah in 1964 as a haven for orphaned and illegally captive Orangutans. Opponents suggest that the money could be better spent exclusively on in situ programmes with wild primates. The consensus, however, is that both programmes have a role, to highlight the primate's plight and to perform valuable educational roles. Any efforts to protect Orangutans are essential as conservationists have warned that the population of 70–100,000 animals has more than halved in the 16 years of their study (1999–2015)

Feeding times at Orangutan rehabilitation centres ensure animal sightings.

Sabah

Danum Valley is where Orangutans live in the wild, but they also move freely through Sepilok Sanctuary on the outskirts of Sandakan, with scheduled feeding slots being the best times to see them. Animals are trained by rangers to fend for themselves. Over time, they become less dependent on the rangers and are released into the wild – more than 100 have been released to date.

Sarawak

In addition to wild Orangutans in Batang Ai National Park, there are two centres near Kuching – Semenggoh Nature Reserve and Matang Wildlife Centre within Kubah National Park. The former is more like Sepilok, while the latter has large enclosures and spacious cages. Crocodiles, bears, cats and bird aviaries are also housed at Matang.

Kalimantan

Tanjung Puting National Park (see pp. 144–145) is a wild Orangutan habitat supporting 4,000 of the species. Three feeding stations are the focus of the tourist programme. These become crowded during the peak season (June and July), but the opportunity to get close to the animals does not deter adventurers. Many travel through the park on double-deck, liveaboard *klotok* boats, with guests on the upper level and the crew on the bottom one. Two- to three-day cruises are popular, and accommodation is also offered at Rimba Eco Lodge.

To the west, the remaining lowland forests of Lamandau Wildlife Reserve of 76,000ha (187,800 acres) support 500 Orangutans. Efforts to secure this habitat are being made by the Orangutan Foundation and its Indonesian counterpart, Yayorin, in partnership with government agencies. Visitors can stay overnight and visit the reserve via Pangkalanbun or Kumai, or in the Yayorin homestay.

Ketapang Orangutan Rehabilitation Centre is located near the town of the same name in West Kalimantan, and rehabilitates Orangutans that have lost their forest habitat. The Orangutan Project is securing large tracts of forest as a primate habitat. Volunteering and adventure-touring opportunities are offered.

Orphaned Orangutans are trained to fend for themselves in rehabilitation centres.

Marine Parks

Borneo's long coastline and surrounding satellite islands are valuable habitats for marine organisms, amphibians and birds, including migratory birds that rest here. Many islands are surrounded by coral reefs, and mangroves are common on the fringes of the land and along estuarine riverbanks.

Sabah

There are several ecologically significant marine parks and islands in the waters of Sabah. The parks include Tun Sakaran Marine Park (off Semporna), Pulau Tiga Park (off Papar) and Tun Mustapha Marine Park (off Kudat).

Being the closest to Kota Kinabalu, Tunku Abdul Rahman Park is the most developed of Sabah's marine parks. Manukan and Gaya Islands provide accommodation, while Sapi has a good beach, snorkelling and a zipline.

Turtle Islands Park, 40km (25 miles) north of Sandakan, is one of the best sites in Borneo to see Green and Hawksbill Turtles, which come onshore nightly to lay eggs. There is a visitors' centre and basic

Lankayan Island Dive Resort off Sandakan offers chalets just metres from the water's edge.

accommodation on Selingan Island that requires advanced booking. Neighbouring Libaran Island has even more rudimentary accommodation.

Lankayan Island is 90 minutes by boat north-east of Sandakan near the maritime border with the Philippines. There is a resort and 32 dive sites, including two small wrecks. Black-tipped Reef Sharks swim in the shallows.

Sipadan is Malaysia's only deep-water island, and it is rated as one of the world's ten best sites for drift diving. Nearby Mabul and Kapalai Islands house global divers who travel daily to Sipadan. Layang-Layang Island within the Spratly Islands and 300km (186 miles) north-west of Kota Kinabalu is another exciting dive island. There is a resort here, and there are several flights a week from Kota Kinabalu on MASwings.

Mantanani Island, three hours' travel north from Kota Kinabalu, comprises three popular day-trip islands, although there is some accommodation and a dive centre. It is also home to a nesting cave of German's Swiftlets, is important for frigatebirds and is the sole Borneo location of the Mantanani Scops Owl. It is also an excellent site for rare island pigeons.

Caution needs to be exercised in some coastal areas such as at Miri.

Sarawak

Sarawak has a few offshore islands as well as some coastal national parks like Bako, Maludam, Similajau and Tanjung Duta.

Talang-Salang National Park comprises four islands off the Sarawak coastline. Two are accessible via Semantan, and the other two from Santubong. This park of 19,414ha (47,973 acres) has protected coastlines and waters for turtle conservation. Female Green Turtles comprise the bulk of the turtles that land here from May to September to lay eggs. Turtle hatcheries protect these eggs before the hatchlings are released. There are no scheduled ferries to the park, and it is best to join an organized tour combined with dolphin watching and mangrove touring.

Kalimantan

Derawan Island in East Kalimantan off Sokan (see pp. 136–137) comprises 31 tropical islands, two of which are settled. Diving around the coral reefs is excellent, while Sangkalaki is Borneo's top turtle-nesting island, as well as a place to sight rare island pigeons.

Gunung Mulu National Park

Gunung Mulu National Park, located in the Sarawak interior and covering 529km² (204 sq miles), is named after Gunung (Mount) Mulu (2,376m/7,795ft). However, it is best known for its subterranean limestone caves, several of which are considered to be among the world's biggest, with Deer, Lang, Wind and Clearwater Caves being the most accessible.

The park is one of two Malaysian UNESCO World Heritage Sites in Borneo, and is protected for its astonishing limestone formations, including caves and karst topography. Visitors travel on boats to reach some of the caves and other park attractions, and to explore a Penan community. Three days is recommended here, with day one focusing on arrival and a visit to Deer and Lang Caves, day two on a visit to Wind and Clearwater Caves, and day three for a canopy walk and departure.

Beneath the Surface

Before Hang Son Doong Cave in Vietnam was discovered in 1991, the caves of Mulu were the hottest contenders for the best caves, with Deer Cave containing the largest passage in the world and Sarawak Chamber the world's largest chamber. Despite being dethroned, the caves of Mulu do not disappoint.

Rooms connected by boardwalk Mulu Marriott

Deer and Lang Caves are only accessible by a long, flat walk (taking one hour) through peat swamp but mostly on an elevated boardwalk. Boardwalks extend across the floors of the caves, which is a good thing given that the ground is an oozing mass of insects consuming mounds of guano (bat droppings).

Above the Surface

After exploring Deer and Lang Caves, most visitors walk to a viewing area in the hope that bats (28 species) will emerge from the caves at dusk. This is an amazing sight, and while the bats are small, the sheer number (in millions) of mostly Wrinkle-lipped Bats emerging from the caves over a few hours has to be seen to be believed. Many of the bats forage over a wide expanse around the park and into neighbouring Brunei (a distance of 65km/40 miles), but they do not emerge when rain is imminent.

It is also possible to climb to the peaks of Mount Api (1,750m/5,741ft) and Mulu, but the three-day exercise should only be undertaken with experienced guides and a good degree of fitness.

Guided walks across the world's longest tree-based canopy walk of 480m (1,575ft), suspended 20m (66ft) above the ground and a stream, are offered several times daily.

The finest accommodation is in the Mulu Marriott Resort and Spa, which has five-star facilities. Chalet and dormitory accommodation is available in the park, and there are some homestays in the village. There are entry fees to the park and it is best to engage the services of a guide.

MASwings operates several flights a

day from its regional hub in Miri, and there are additional but less frequent flights from Kota Kinabalu and Kuching. Some adventurous travellers arrive by road and boat, a journey that takes most of the day from Miri.

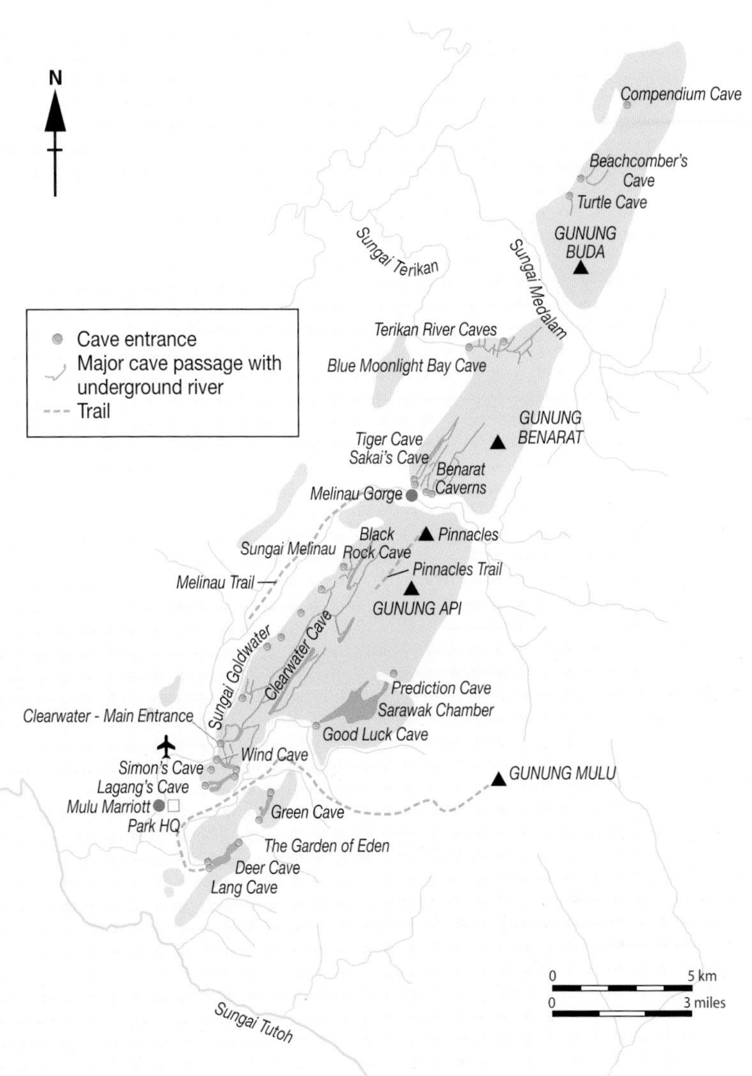

Gunung Mulu National Park.

Bako National Park

Bako National Park is popular for many reasons, including its proximity to Kuching (one hour), and its variety of plant communities, access to wildlife and picturesque coastal setting.

Established in 1957, Bako is situated beside the South China Sea. Compared to most parks in Sarawak and Borneo it is small at just 27km^2 (10 sq miles), yet despite this it has long fascinated conservationists and botanists due to its ecological diversity.

Rivers and Coasts

Boats for the park depart from the well-organized Kampung Bako Jetty. Observant passengers may see crocodiles on the banks, and once out of the river mouth and in the open sea dolphins may be sighted.

Mangroves line the bay, and sandstone cliffs and rocky headlands guard the beach at Teluk Assam, where the park headquarters are located. Millions of years of erosion have sculpted unique formations such as sea arches and stacks just off the coast. Traces of iron minerals in the parent rock have produced layers of hardened pink rock. The sandstone also displays unusual honeycomb weathering that gives the rock its unique texture and appearance.

Forest Communities

Bako supports almost all major plant communities found in Borneo in a single location. It is considered a miniature botanical garden, and those interested in discovering some of Malaysia's bizarre botanical botany will visit Bako. Plant communities include peat-swamp, mangrove, heath and mixed dipterocarp forests.

Rocky headlands and sea stacks of yellow sandstone greet visitors to Bako National Park.

Estuarine crocodiles can be sighted along riverbanks into the park.

Walking one or more of the 16 trails is the most popular activity. The trails are all colour coded and take from between two hours to two days to complete; they are all well signposted and well maintained. There are about 30km (19 miles) of trails altogether, and those planning to walk them all need to allocate a few days to this activity.

On the plateaus the vegetation changes to a heath-like scrub (*kerangas*) that is drier, lower and has a more open canopy than the tropical rainforest. Carnivorous plants such as pitcher plants and sundews thrive here. Observant visitors should spot various primates, especially around the park headquarters, where they have become acclimatized to humans. Long-tailed Macaques are common, while Silvered Langurs are hardly noticeable. Proboscis Monkeys forage among the mangroves, especially around Telok Paku, Telok Delima and Ulu Assam. Colugos, while difficult to locate, also inhabit the forest near the park headquarters.

Facilities

The facilities at Telok Assam are more than adequate, including both a restaurant and a shop selling basic supplies. While what visitors will encounter is far from gourmet dining, it is more than adequate (cooking is not permitted in the chalets). Proper storage of food is important, as the Long-tailed Macaques can be a nuisance around the park headquarters.

Accommodation ranges from premium forest lodges with attached toilet and bathroom plus air-conditioning, to hostel beds with shared bathrooms and fans. Camping is also possible for those who are self contained.

Food and Drink

One of the joys of travel includes eating new dishes and enjoying local beverages. Borneo does not disappoint in this respect, with its many tantalizing tropical products like fruits, vegetables, spices and wild meats. However, it is not only the food but the places where it is purchased and consumed that make Borneo unique.

Staples, Markets and Customs

Rice is the staple ingredient and seafood the main source of protein, especially in coastal areas. Rice is grown as *padi* (flooded field) or *swidden* (upland rice and rain dependent). Several varieties are grown, with Bario rice from the Sarawak highlands being highly prized. Along with Sarawak black pepper, Bario rice is a gourmet product sought by discerning global connoisseurs.

Buying fresh produce is important especially in Borneo's smaller locations, where morning and night markets (*pasar malam*) are popular. In the cities, night markets may be held in different venues on different nights. In some places markets are called *tamu*, and most have a 'wet' and a 'dry' area – meat, vegetables, fish and fruits are sold in the former. Refrigeration is mostly non-existent, but markets only last a few hours.

Markets selling fresh produce are the best places to see exotic fruits and vegetables, such as these ginger flowers and soursop.

It is important for travellers to appreciate that Muslims eat and serve *halal* food (meat slaughtered according to Muslim law) and that alcohol is not available in certain places, especially in Brunei. Many restaurants close in the daylight hours during the fasting month of Ramadan. However, neighbouring communities may hunt wild pigs and drink *tuak* (rice wine), so it is always best to ask before offending local sensibilities.

Food styles in Sarawak and Sabah follow the country's main racial groups of Malay, Chinese and Indian, although Indian food is not as well represented as it is in Peninsular Malaysia. Added to this are dishes from tribal communities and some Filipino influences in parts of Sabah. Another complexity is that there is no one Chinese or Malay style, but rather a multitude of regional variations.

Stalls, Warungs and Snacks

The people of Borneo enjoy hawker food (*warung*), while city dwellers can also seek out global cuisines, particularly in shopping mall food courts.

Snacking is common, with many people eating five small meals of breakfast, lunch, tea, dinner and supper. Short breaks are often taken in coffee shops – in Sarawak and Sabah, *teh tarik* (local tea) is the preferred beverage, though it is also possible to order *caffe latte* in branded outlets. Borneo-grown coffee from places like Tenom in Sabah is becoming increasingly recognized.

Acclaimed Dishes

Spices, chilli, garlic, coconut milk, onions, lemongrass, ginger and *sambal* (spicy chilli sauce) are important ingredients in many dishes.

Some well-known dishes include *laksa* (spicy noodle soup), *beef rendang* (spicy beef), *mee goring* (fried noodles), *nasi kandar/padang* (rice smorgasbord) and *satay* (meat on skewers grilled over charcoal flames). There are many variations on these dishes, with Sarawak *laksa*, for example, being the favourite in that state.

Football-sized, spiky durians ('the king of fruits'), giant red bananas, wild starfruit and *salak* (snake fruit) are some of the unusual fruits that are available.

Delicious Borneo Delicacies

Fruits
Bambangan (wild mango)
Jungle durian (durian isu)
Ba 'Kelalan Apples
Salak (snake fruit)
Sarawak pineapples

Vegetables
Sayur manis (leafy green vegetable)
Midin (fern)
Sarawak black pepper

From the Sea
Seafood
Latok (seaweed eaten by the Bajau)

Crops
Sago
Bario rice

Beverages
Tuak (rice wine)
Tenom Coffee
Sabah tea

Dishes
Bird's nest soup
Sago worms
Hinava/Umai (raw fish 'cooked' in lime juice
Sarawak kolok mee (noodles)
Sarawak laksa (spicy noodle soup)
Manok pansoh (chicken cooked in bamboo)
Tebaloi (sago-based snack)
Layered cake)

Satay sticks grilled on charcoal fires are a common street food in most parts of Borneo.

PART 2: AROUND BORNEO

Borneo includes the Malaysian states of Sarawak and Sabah, the Sultanate of Brunei and the Indonesian territory of Kalimantan. Ancient trade routes connected the island's coastal areas like Kota Kinabalu, Sabah (pictured) and opened them up to outsiders.

Kota Kinabalu at sunset.

Introduction to Sabah

Sabah includes the two substantive islands of Banggi and Balambangan to the north offshore from Kudat. Labuan on the east coast is not part of Sabah, but is administered as a federal territory by the Malaysian government. Its south-west border adjoins Sarawak, while its southern border is shared with North Kalimantan. The Dent Peninsula occupies the east of Sabah, and the famous diving island of Sipadan is offshore from Semporna.

Covering 72,500km^2 (28,000 sq miles), Sabah is home to 3.5 million people. Kota Kinabalu is the biggest city and the state capital, with 207,214 residents. The next largest city is Sandakan, with a population of 157,330.

Sabah is culturally diverse, comprising people from local tribes and those from around the region, including Peninsular Malaysia, China, the Philippines and Indonesia. The locals include Kadazan-Dusun, Rungus, Bajau, Murut and Suluk.

Transport

Kota Kinabalu is an international gateway with direct flights from several regional destinations, as well as from Peninsular Malaysia. There are also direct flights from Peninsular Malaysia to Sandakan, Tawau and Labuan, and domestic flights to other places in Sabah and Borneo. While it is possible to use public transport, many people choose to save time and fly within Sabah to destinations such as Sandakan, Lahad Datu, Tawau and Kudat, as well as Labuan.

Car hire is available, but be aware that many roads are not major ones and are used by a variety of vehicles, including slow-moving agricultural ones.

River transport, apart from that along the Kinabatangan and Menanggul, is not as important as it is in Sarawak and Kalimantan. However, ferries and boats are the only way to access offshore tourist spots such as Turtle Islands, Sipadan/Mabul/Kapalai Islands, Lankayan Island, Tiga Island and Mantanani Island. There is a ferry service to Labuan Island from Kota Kinabalu and Brunei.

Kota Kinabalu Waterfront.

Planning

The main attractions in Kota Kinabalu can be seen in two days. Three days should be allocated to climbing Mount Kinabalu (arrival the night before, an overnight rest on the mountain and one night to recover from the climb). Sandakan requires one full day, while Turtle Islands is best done over two days and the Kinabatangan River over three days. Visiting Lahad Datu, Danum Valley and the Tabin Wildlife Reserve requires at least five days to make all the travel worthwhile.

Sabah is situated in the tropics, and has a hot and moist climate that is affected by two monsoon seasons – the north-east and the south-west. The north-east monsoon (November to April) brings heavy rains, while the south-west monsoon (May to September) is drier. Like most tropical areas, the rain tends to fall in short and intense bursts, and not long after the rain stops and life returns to normal.

The key destinations to visit in Sabah are Kota Kinabalu, Mount Kinabalu, Sandakan (for Sepilok, Turtle Islands and Kinabatangan River), Lahad Datu (Tabin Wildlife Reserve and Danum Valley), and Tawau (Tawau Hills, Maliau Basin and Sipadan).

Sepilok's Rainforest Discovery Centre.

Kota Kinabalu

Formerly known as Jesselton (after Sir Charles Jessel of the North Borneo Chartered Company), the Sabah state capital of Kota Kinabalu ('KK') is a picturesque coastal city situated by the South China Sea and with the islands of Tunku Abdul Rahman Park located just offshore. On a clear day Mount Kinabalu can be seen off in the distance, 90km (56 miles) away. The foothills to the Crocker Range rise just beyond the city limits.

Kota Kinabalu became the capital of British North Borneo, then Sabah, after the Second World War because it had been less affected by Allied bombing than the then capital of Sandakan whose commercial heart had been completely destroyed by Allied bombs in their efforts to dislodge Japanese forces.

Some 463,000 people live in the capital, but this figure increases to almost 900,000 when surrounding districts are included. It has a complex cultural mix, with perhaps 20 per cent of the population classified as non-Malaysians (mostly Filipino). Tourism is important but the city is also the state's commercial and industrial centre.

While the seashore and beaches of Kota Kinabalu are not spectacular, those on the islands of Tunku Abdul Rahman

Sutera Harbour is an integrated resort along the Kota Kinabalu waterfront.

Park (see pp. 36–37) are far better, with Sapi Island being a popular retreat for day trippers. Gaya Island is home to a large over-the-water community, as well as two resorts of international standard. There is also a substantial mangrove forest on the island. Manukan Island houses the park headquarters and a collection of sea-facing chalets. Snorkelling and some diving are done around the islands in the park.

City Attractions

Visitors can obtain a good view of the city from Signal Hill, which is just a 20-minute climb from the city. It is also a great place from which to watch White-bellied Sea-eagles and Brahminy Kites soar high over the city and the South China Sea.

The Sabah State Museum is a repository for the state's cultural artefacts and records of its natural history. The original museum opened in Gaya Street in 1965 due to the hard efforts of the Sabah Society. It occupied its new site in 1984 and includes distinctive architecture, defined as vernacular revivalism since it is based on a Rungus longhouse with a broad, sloping roof covering outwards-sloping walls. It contains valuable historic records and photographs, as well as ceramics and brassware. There is a lake in the surrounding gardens where traditional tribal dwellings such as a Kadazan-Dusun bamboo house can be seen in the Heritage Village. The museum is a one-stop cultural centre with the adjoining Education and Science Centre, plus the Sabah Art Gallery.

Two other cultural attractions, at Mari Mari Cultural Village and Monsopiad Heritage Village, are located in suburban Kota Kinabalu.

Mari Mari offers a forested setting and an insight into the cultures of traditional communities of the Bajau, Lundayeh (or Lun Bawang), Rungus, Murut and Kadazan-Dusun. Visitors can watch blowpipe displays, dances and tattooing, sample food and learn more about the mythical beliefs of the community. Three tours are offered throughout the day.

It is the House of Skulls at Monsopiad Heritage Village that lures most visitors. Named after a legendary headhunter, it provides a valuable opportunity to learn about the famous Kadazan-Dusun tribal elder and the way of life of his people, then and today. Visitors can investigate a granary, the headman's house and, of course, some trophy skulls of the former headhunter warrior. Monsopiad is located 16km (10 miles) south of Kota Kinabalu.

There are several mosques in the city, with the most impressive being Sabah State Mosque and the City Mosque at Likas, the latter giving the appearance of floating on the lake that it adjoins. It was built in 2000 and is reported to be able to accommodate up to 12,000 worshippers.

Natural Wetlands

Large areas of wetland once lined the Kota Kinabalu waterfront, but most have now been reclaimed in a city where there is limited flat land for urban growth. As late as the 1990s, water villages with houses built on stilts above the water still existed in the mid-downtown parts of the city. The villagers were relocated and the land reclaimed for mostly commercial use.

Likas Wetlands and the nearby Kota Kinabalu Bird Sanctuary to the north of the city are havens for resident and migratory birds from North Asia. These coastal wetlands are also a valuable breeding ground for marine organisms and are protected by the Department of Fisheries

Fishing boats and ferries moor along the Kota Kinabalu waterfront.

Sabah. There have also been rare sightings of the Nankeen Night Heron and Lesser Adjutant Stork in this wetland.

Kota Kinabalu Bird Sanctuary is a large expanse of remnant mangroves and brackish pools, which are accessible via boardwalks extending for more than 1.4km (1 mile). An information centre provides background on the flora and fauna. There is a nesting colony of Purple Herons that can be seen from a hide, while Little and Intermediate Egrets feed among the mangroves. Striated Herons, Blue-eared Kingfishers, Blue-throated Bee-eaters and Greenshanks may also be sighted in the sanctuary.

Waterfront

The strip from Likas in the north to Tanjung Aru in the south serves various functions, including recreational parks, wetlands, the city centre and coastal resorts with adjoining golf courses. The KK Waterfront is where a lot of the city's dining and entertainment occurs, with restaurants, pubs and cafes situated along a raised wooden boardwalk.

Sutera Harbour Resort is also situated on reclaimed land. This integrated complex includes two hotels, a marina, a golf course, restaurants, bars and a housing estate. The adjoining mudflats are good for birdwatching.

Visitors can enjoy sea breezes and vistas of the five islands scattered off the coast from many coastal locations, with Tanjung Aru being one of the best. The locals take up positions at the many food stalls beneath towering casuarina trees in Prince Philip Park, while the more upmarket location is the adjoining five-star resort.

Markets

Gaya Street Market is held every Sunday morning on one of the city's main streets and is the most popular open-air market. While locals seek out pots, pans, plastic buckets, fresh fruits and vegetables, and 'cure-alls' from a medicine man, tourists are more interested in the many souvenir stalls (for t-shirts, jewellery and beadwork). Restaurants line the street, some doing a lively early morning trade selling *dim sum* to locals who come for the Sunday street theatre as much as for the produce sold.

The waterfront Filipino Market (officially Pasar Kraftangan) is also popular with tourists, and though prices are cheap, haggling is expected. Anything and everything is sold, from clothes, sarongs and bags, to seafood products. These markets are also a great venue to get running repairs and alterations on clothing at one of the many sewing-machine operators situated along the front entrance. Despite the name, not everything is Filipino, with many souvenirs originating from Indonesia and China. Very few items these days are hand-made, most of the items are mass-produced.

Shopping malls are especially popular with the locals, who enjoy making a day of visiting places such as Plaza 333, Api-Api Centre, Centre Point, Wisma Merdeka and 1 Borneo for eating, entertainment and drinking, as well as shopping.

In the evening visitors can enjoy the night food market that adjoins the wet market along the waterfront, and a more traditional night market (Sinsuran Market or Pasar Malam Sinsuran) in a nearby street called Jalan Kamunta.

Getting There

Kota Kinabalu Airport is a regional and domestic hub with direct international flights to several neighbouring countries, as well as to the offshore islands of Labuan and Layang-Layang. It is Malaysia's second busiest airport after Kuala Lumpur.

Ferries to Labuan and the offshore islands depart from Jesselton Point and other locations such as in front of the Hyatt Regency Kinabalu Hotel near the city centre.

Where to Stay

Sutera Harbour Resort
www.suteraharbour.com
Gayana Marine Resort
(www.echoresorts.com)
Gaya Island Resort
(www.gayaislandresort.com)
Hyatt Regency Hotel
www.regency.hyatt.com

Sunday's Gaya Street Market is popular with both tourists and locals.

South of Kota Kinabalu

The land to the south and south-west of Kota Kinabalu is located between the South China Sea and the Crocker Range National Park. Urban Kota Kinabalu extends part of the way south, then it is agricultural land or forests for much of the way to the Sarawak border. Agricultural crops include rice, rubber, oil palm, pineapples and mangoes. One of the exciting ways to discover the south-west is via the train to Tenom or via the ferry to the island of Labuan.

Train to Tenom

Passenger trains operated by Sabah State Railway travel from Tanjung Aru to Tenom (140km/87 miles) via Beaufort. This is an exciting journey for train buffs, as the railway on the Beaufort to Tenom sector passes along the edge of the rainforest lining the Padas River.

Many visitors catch a bus or van to Beaufort, then join the train, but the whole journey is recommended. Dedicated trainspotters will catch the train to Tenom, stay the night and catch the return train the next morning, otherwise it becomes too rushed given the many things to see in Tenom. Another alternative is to catch the bus to or from Tenom, and travel the other leg on the train.

During colonial times the train transported produce to market, as well as providing a lifeline for those who lived in Sabah's south-west. Even today it still serves a valuable function, carrying people and goods to and from Tenom (the train originally went further north-east of Tenom to the town of Melalap, but this section has been abandoned). Tourists can get an idea of the days of the Chartered Company and the British Colonial Office, when young Englishmen set off on their tropical adventures as planters and plantation managers in the mystical Far East.

The local train from Kota Kinabalu to Tenom passes through the scenic Padas Valley.

The route of the passenger train.

The public train is not only cheap, but full of character and characters. On odd occasions – when there is a delay such as a landslide – it can take up to six hours to reach its destination.

The journey from Tenom to Beaufort is a scenic journey mostly along the banks of the Padas River which flows freely until a hydro-electric plant on the river all but stops the flow of water. The train stops at stations that are little more than bus stop shelters where farmers appear with bags of produce to take to the markets in Beaufort and Papar. At Pangi Station, the rear car of the two-car diesel train is positioned to the front before the train continues its journey. At Halogilat Station, two hours into the journey, passengers alight and join a new train with a few more carriages.

Just outside Tenom there is an excellent agricultural research station with an extensive selection of tropical plants. This remote 200ha (494-acre) park supports many colourful tropical plants, especially orchids and commercial crop species. Known as Taman Pertanian Sabah, it includes an orchid house and a research centre for tropical plants like cacao, coffee and fruit species. Such is the assemblage of plants that celebrated naturalist Sir David Attenborough once filmed here. The park is open daily except on Mondays, and is located some 15km (9 miles) north-east of Tenom in Lagud Seberang. Sampling the local coffee is an essential activity in Tenom.

Tenom Fatt Choi, one of the district's leading commercial coffee producers, has established a very inviting concept outlet in the town where their coffee is served and the beans sold.

North Borneo Steam Train

The North Borneo Steam Train (operated by Sutera Harbour Resort) is a nostalgic tourist train runing from KK to Papar and back. It operates on Wednesdays and Saturdays, departing mid-morning and returning in the early afternoon, and is substantially more expensive than the regular Tenom train, but lunch and beverages are included.

The steam locomotive travels from Tanjung Aru in the south of Kota Kinabalu, recreating the initial journey that commenced in 1896. The carriages have been refurbished to simulate the colonial era, with both the exteriors and interiors reflecting the ambience of the 19th century. There is no air-conditioning, and ceiling fans keep the train cool. The exterior is painted in the traditional racing green and cream of the original train, and a brass logo features the original design of a tiger standing on the royal crown while holding a rail wheel. Fuelled by local *baku* logs sourced from mangrove forests, the locomotive is thought to be one of the few trains left in the world that still utilizes forest timber.

This tourist train dates back to 2000 and is a joint venture between Sutera Harbour Resort and the Sabah State Railway. It accommodates 80 passengers in five carriages hauled by an 82-tonne steam locomotive engine made by the Vulcan Foundry in Lancashire, UK.

The rail line proceeds from Tanjung Aru through to Kinarut, then Papar. A Buddhist temple in Kinarut is the first of several stops along the way. It is a colourful Buddhist structure, and tourists can enjoy the opportunity for a closer look at it.

While the track passes inland from coastal Kinarut, there are some very pleasant resorts along the casuarina-lined beach here, plus one situated on Dinawan Island a few kilometres offshore.

The train then continues past mangroves and rice fields. It crosses the Papar River over a steel trestle bridge leading into the town for a 40-minute stop to enable passengers to experience the local market. While the passengers visit the market, the train is turned on a huge wheel for the return journey.

On the way back drinks and lunch are served by the crew decked out with pith-helmets to replicate the colonial times. Lunch is delivered in *tiffin* boxes, as it would have been in those days.

Rafting the Padas River

White-water rafting is possible on the Padas and Kiulu Rivers. The Padas is hot by name and hot by nature. While the water

Whitewater rafting on the Kiulu River.

looks chocolate-brown, an exhilarating ride is guaranteed on up to grade four rafting conditions. Travelling to the departure point is half the fun, as rafters have to get up at sunrise to catch the train from Beaufort to Pangi Station on the way to Tenom. From here, it is a 14-km (7-mile) raft trip back down the river to Rayoh Station. Rafters then rejoin the train for the return journey to Beaufort and on to Kota Kinabalu.

Where to Stay

Langkah Syabas Beach Resort
(www.langkahsyabas.com.my)
Sunborneo Island Resort
(www.sunborneo.com.my)

Klias Peninsula and Offshore Islands

The two main island groups off the south-west coast of Sabah are the Tiga and Labuan Islands. The Tiga Islands group consists of a few unsettled islands known as Pulau Tiga National Park. There is a back-to-basics resort on the main island, and one of the islands is renowned for its snakes. There are some low mud volcanoes, too, along with birdlife and wildlife such as monkeys and lizards. The islands became famous as the setting for the first of the *Survivor* series of reality televisions shows.

The departure point for Tiga Island is Kuala Penyu on the Klias Peninsula, about two-hours' drive south-west of the capital. It is an 18-km (11-mile) sea journey from the small port to the islands.

The Klias Peninsula supports the largest stand of mangrove and brackish/freshwater swamp forests in West Sabah. Proboscis Monkeys and Silvered Langurs can be seen on boat tours through the mangroves, and fireflies are evident in the evening.

Kinarut is home to the colourful Tien Nam Shi Buddhist Temple

Labuan

While not part of Sabah, the Federal Territory of Labuan lies just off the state's far south-west coast. These days Labuan is a trade-free zone and tax-free haven, and an International Offshore Financial Centre. It was once part of the Sultanate of Brunei but was ceded to the British in 1846. James Brooke, the first Rajah of Sarawak, was also the Governor of Labuan. There was once a suggestion that Labuan would become the next Singapore but this has never materialized.

Its capital is officially Victoria but there are very few references to this and no-one on the island would refer to the main commercial area by this name, calling it simply Bandar Labuan or Labuan Town. In 1984, the Sabah Government ceded the island to the Malaysian Federal Government and it is now administered as a federal territory. Some 100,000 residents call Labuan home.

The British were attracted here by coal to fuel the steamships that were then plying the oceans. Seven companies mined the coal for 64 years and there was a railway line from the mines at Tanjung Kubong to Victoria Port. Coal was depleted by 1911 but fishing and shipbuilding ensured that the local economy continued to flourish. Today, the island's economy is driven by the ship repair yard that provides repair and maintenance facilities for the vessels that service the flourishing offshore oil and gas industry. It is also the home of the Labuan International Business and Financial Centre which was established in 1990 to support offshore banking..

For some international visitors, Labuan is close to their hearts as it played a strategic regional role in the Second World War. Japanese forces occupied Labuan from 1941 to 1945 and renamed the island Pulau Maida after their commanding officer. The liberation of Borneo by Australian troops from the 9th Division started in Labuan in June 1945 under the high command of General Douglas MacArthur. A plaque in front of the small Labuan Museum marks the place where the Australian forces landed.

At the cessation of the war, the Japanese surrendered to the Allied forces on Labuan. Other places of military interest around the island include the Surrender Point, Peace

Dam and Clubhouse at the Labuan golf course.

Grand Dorsett Labuan and Financial Centre.

Park and Labuan War Cemetery where the remains of Allied soldiers are buried.

Labuan is billed as the 'Island of Gardens' and is a reasonably decent place to rest for a few days. It has several good hotels, plenty of seafood restaurants and a lively night life in various locations. A nine-hole golf course on the island is also well patronized; visitors are very welcome to enjoy a round of golf, and a cool drink and meal after their game.

While perhaps not for serious birdwatchers, the Labuan Bird Park (Taman Burung Labuan) near The Chimney at Tanjung Kubong has three large enclosures housing some of the birds of Borneo as well as some from offshore such as Ostriches, Macaws and various species of parrot

The main island is surrounded by six smaller ones and offshore shipwrecks that have put the area on the map with divers, along with several other interesting dive sites, such as Vernon Bank, which offers the possibility of sighting rare marine species like the porcelain crab. Three islands (Kuraman, Rusakan Kecil and Rusakan Besar) make up Labuan Marine Park.

Visitors also come to Labuan to enjoy its beaches and duty-free shopping.

Getting There

Labuan is 10 km (6.2 miles) south-east of the Sabah coast and 25 km (15.5 miles) north of Brunei. There are direct flights to Labuan from Kuala Lumpur on Peninuslar Malaysia, Kota Kinabalu and Kuching.

Where to Stay

Dorsett Grand Labuan
(www.dorsetthotels.com)
Tiara Labuan Hotel
(www.tiaralabuan.com)
Survivor Lodge Pulau Tiga
(www.sdclodges.com)
Palm Beach Resort and Spa Labuan
(www.palmbeachresortspa.com)

Kota Kinabalu: North to Kudat

The road north from Kota Kinabalu all the way to Kudat and the northernmost tip of Borneo is one that is less travelled by tourists. Once out of the capital, it is a very relaxing journey of 175km (109 miles) that takes about three hours, mostly along rural roads. For those in a hurry, there are daily flights to and from Kudat and Sandakan on MASwings.

Kudat became the capital of what was known in the 19th century as British North Borneo. The region became of commercial interest to the British when oil was discovered there in the late 19th century. Kudat was officially founded in 1881 and declared the capital in 1882. It did not remain the capital for long, however, with

The northernmost tip of Borneo is 215km (134 miles) north of Kota Kinabalu.

The Black-crowned Night Heron frequents wetlands.

Sandakan replacing it in 1884. Access was difficult and until the 1960s, when a road was built, the only way in and out was by sea.

Coastal Drive

There are several beachside resorts with adjoining golf courses along the coast just north of Kota Kinabalu. Nexus Karambunai Resort has a golf course that offers good birdwatching sites, especially for herons and egrets that roost in the mangrove trees lining small creeks. Nearby, there are two water villages at Mengkabong and Penimbawan, where Bajau people live in houses built on stilts perched over the water.

Tuaran is just one hour north of the capital, with Dalit Bay being the location for the Shangri-la Rasa Ria Resort and adjoining golf course. Both occupy a prime position along the casuarina-lined beachfront. Mangroves once stood where the golf course now is, and there are still some mangroves lining the adjoining streams. These are home to birds such as Purple Herons, Collared Kingfishers, Oriental Honey-buzzards, Blue-throated Bee-eaters and Brahminy Kites.

Sabah's northern beaches are one of Borneo's best-kept secrets.

Markets, Cowboys and Longhouses

At Tuaran the main road heads north to Kota Belud, which is the halfway point on the journey to Kudat. The Bajau tribes of Kota Belud are known as the Cowboys of the East and are recognized for their horse-riding abilities. Each Sunday from 6 a.m. to 2 p.m. the local market is a colourful and mostly local affair. The annual Tamu Besar Kota Belud is the biggest market of the year and a day of special festivities.

Birdwatchers can deviate westwards from the main road and head towards the coast, especially from late October to early March, to sight migratory raptors heading from here to Palawan in the Philippines. The road continues on to the departure point for Mantanani Island (see p. 37).

Long, uninhabited stretches of white sandy beach, farming land and forested foothills extend all the way north. There is not much else in the area apart from rice fields, coconut and banana plantations, and a few isolated farmhouses.

This is the territory of the Rungus, who were formerly regarded as a sub-group of the Kadazan-Dusun but have more recently been considered a full ethnic group. Their culture revolves around rice cultivation,

The northern tip of Sabah (and Borneo) is lined with long stretches of untouched beaches.

and while many Rungus now work in towns, some still live in their traditional longhouses. Longhouses of more than 75 doors were apparently once common, but they now rarely exceed ten. It is said that a Rungus *bobolizan* (witch doctor) can communicate with the spirits, and some still conduct their traditional duties of curing the sick and performing rituals. A longhouse at Kampung Bavanggazo, 41km (25 miles) south of Kudat, can be visited.

Kudat and the Tip of Borneo

Situated near the northernmost tip of Borneo, few Malaysian destinations are as remote as Kudat. However, it is the isolation that is the main reason why people make the effort to travel all the way to this farflung outpost of civilization.

Considering its northern location, it is not surprising that Kudat was one of the first parts of Sabah to be settled by Chinese immigrants, in particular the Hakka dialect people (from various parts of southern China including Guangdong, Fujian, Sichuan and Hainan Provinces). Most of these were also Christians. The first group arrived in 1883 having received assisted passage from the British North Borneo Chartered Company. They were brought in to work the land and develop the region, and were given free land, tools and limited rations to tide them over for a few months upon their arrival.

Kudat, with a population of 30,000, is home to Sabah's oldest golf course. There is a comfortable resort and marina situated near the centre of the small town.

Head north from the small port of Kudat and apart from the even more remote Malaysian outpost of Pulau Banggi, it is open water all the way across the Sulu Sea to Palawan Island in the Philippines.

Kudat is one of Borneo's best-kept beachside secrets, where long sandy beaches, rolling surf, foothills with commanding views and untouched coastal rainforests remain much as they have for the past centuries.

The Tip of Borneo (at Tanjung Simpang Mengayau, a 30-minute drive north of Kudat) near Matunggong, has been developed into a low-key tourist attraction. Although the beachfront is very scenic, there is little else to do here but pose under the Malaysian flag or swim along the deserted coastline of the South China/Sulu Seas. Various longhouses of the Rungus people can be visited, and some offer an extended homestay programme.

This is another excellent location to sight migratory raptors which fly over between the peak months of late October to early March. Look out for the Oriental Honey-buzzard, Peregrine Falcon, Osprey, Grey-faced Buzzard, Japanese Sparrowhawk and Chinese Goshawk.

A total of 244 bird species is recorded as migrants or vagrants to Borneo. It has been estimated that maybe 15 million birds reach Borneo each year from North Asia and as far away as Siberia. Birds that breed in the north migrate southwards from September to November, and return from March to May. Birds that breed in Australia migrate northwards through Borneo from April to May, returning in August and September.

Where to Stay

Nexus Karambunai Resort (www.nexusresort.com)
Shangri-La Rasa Ria Resort (www.shangri-la.com)
Kudat Golf and Marina Resort (www.kudatgolfmarina.com)

The Crocker Ranges and the Mountainous West

Mount Kinabalu (see pp. 32–33) looms in the distance, and is so high that it can be seen from Kota Kinabalu 80km (50 miles) away. While it and its surrounding park are one of the main reasons why many people travel to Sabah, there are other attractions in and around the mountainous ranges on Sabah's west coast.

Crocker Range National Park is located south-west of Mount Kinabalu, while Mount Trus Madi lies due south. There is limited cabin accommodation in the Crocker Ranges at Mahua Visitors Centre in the north and the park headquarters in the south-west near Keningau.

Dairies are rare in the tropics, but the relatively cool climate of the Mount Kinabalu foothills provides an ideal environment for the dairy in Mesilau, near Kundasang. The grassy paddocks of Desa Dairy Farm cover the rolling hills here, and visitors can participate in interactive farming activities and sample dairy products. For golfers seeking both altitude and attitude, the Mount Kinabalu Golf Course adjoining the dairy is one of Southeast Asia's highest courses. The 18-hole, par 72 course is situated at 1,500m (4,931ft) with Mount Kinabalu views.

Kundasang is located just 6km (3.7 miles) from Kinabalu Park and is famous for its markets, which feature temperate vegetables and flowers. Chalet accommodation here and along the mountain ridge to the park offers an alternative to that offered in the park.

Poring Hot Springs are a popular place to swim and relax.

Poring Hot Springs are positioned on the eastern side of Kinabalu Park, and the pools of steaming spring water are the perfect place for recovering from the mountain ascent. Water is piped into Japanese-style baths, and while some visitors come for the healthy properties of the sulphur-enriched waters, most just visit for relaxation and family picnics.

Not far from the pools there is the possibility of a range of nature-based activities, involving trails, waterfalls, a butterfly farm, caves, orchid gardens and a canopy walk through the uppermost layers of the rainforest. The canopy walk is designed for scientific research and public recreation.

White-water rafting is possible on the gently flowing Kiulu River located just south of Tamparuli. The main road to Mount Kinabalu passes through Tamparuli near Tuaran, although there is a longer and alternate route via Kota Belud. The road from the park continues eastwards to Kundasang, Ranau (there is a tea farm and resort just beyond the town), Beluran and Sandakan.

Giant Flowers

As mentioned earlier (see p. 25), the rafflesia plant produces the world's biggest flowers. It takes months to bloom and the flowers only last about three days before decomposing. Located one hour south from Kota Kinabalu near Tambunan (join a tour, self-drive or catch a local van/bus), the Rafflesia Information Centre is the best place to see the flowers, as the rangers can locate them within the forest. Expect to walk between 15 and 90 minutes to reach the flowers, and ring ahead to ensure that some are in bloom.

The road from Tambunan continues south-west to Keningau, where it branches with the western road continuing on to Tenom, and the southeastern road heading below the Maliau Basin and on to Tawau on the east coast.

Golfers at Mount Kinabalu Golf Course can admire the towering mountain from most holes.

Where to Stay

Perkasa Hotel Kundasang
(www.perkasahotel.com.my)
Sutera Sanctuary Lodges
(www.suterasanctuarylodges.com

Sandakan and its Offshore Islands

Sandakan is the gateway to the north-east of Sabah and provides access to sights in and around the city, several offshore islands, and also the Kinabatangan River and Gomantong Caves.

Sabah's second largest city of 156,000 residents was once the capital of British North Borneo, but after being extensively bombed during the Second World War, the capital was relocated to Jesselton (later renamed Kota Kinabalu).

Several European powers showed early interest in Sandakan; eventually, in 1879, it became a port and settlement administered by the British North Borneo Chartered Company.

Buying fish at the Sandakan Central Market.

City Attractions

Sandakan's centre is worth visiting despite the fact that most of its historic buildings were destroyed at the end of the war.

Puu Jih Shih Buddhist Temple on the summit above Tanah Merah shines in the early morning light. Built in 1987, it is a dazzling red-and-gold structure adorned with threatening dragons and swastikas. It's also a good spot for views of Sandakan Bay.

Sandakan Central Market is one of Malaysia's most colourful markets due to the presence of many local ethnic groups, as well as itinerant Filipino and Indonesian workers. Some of these people live in one of several water villages that extend into Sandakan Bay. Not surprisingly, there is a large fish and seafood section.

Sandakan is big enough to support a few large hotels that deliver international standards, as well as many smaller local ones offering warm Malaysian hospitality. Some line the western shore of the expansive harbour.

Guests really have to pinch themselves to be reminded that they are indeed in the wilds of Sabah as they partake of scones, clotted cream, jam and tea, while playing a spot of croquet on the lawns of an old house perched on Trig Hill above Sandakan Bay. The English Tea House and Restaurant could easily be the setting for a Somerset Maugham novel and is one of the last bastions of colonialism. It is a suitable venue to recover from an adventurous tour of the nearby Orangutan Sanctuary or the wetlands of the Kinabatangan floodplain.

Afterwards, visitors can take a stroll up the road to the Agnes Keith House to learn about Sandakan in the 1930s and '40s. American author Agnes Keith wrote several books here, including *Land Below the Wind*.

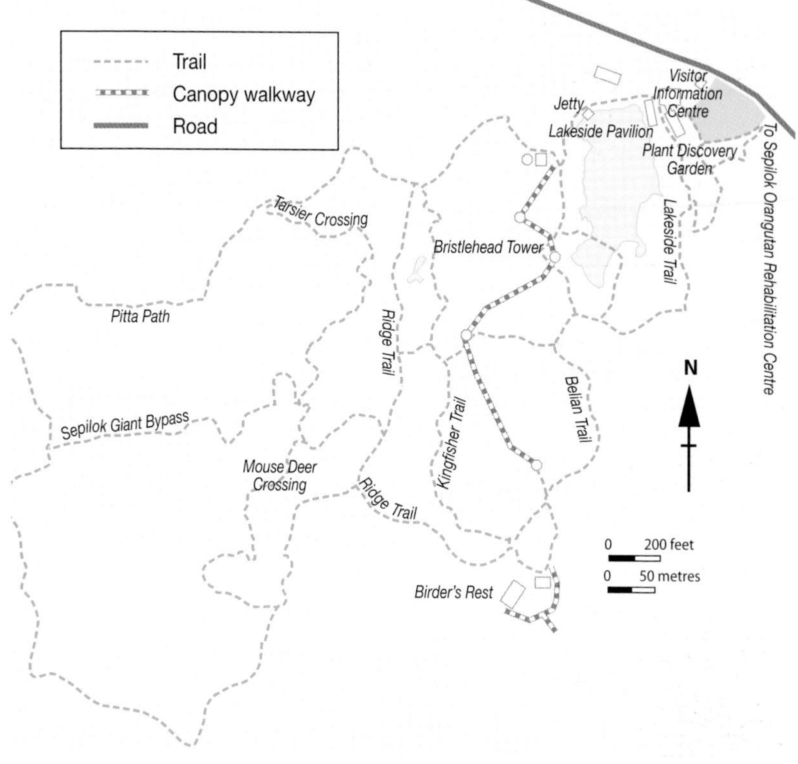

Trails through the Rainforest Discovery Centre at Sepilok.

Out of Town

Another grim reminder of the Second World War is the Sandakan Memorial Park situated on the former Tamba Rimba Prisoner of War Camp at the outskirts of the city. The notorious camp is infamously known as the place where the Death March commenced (see p. 15). There were actually three marches staged between January and March 1945. An excellent interpretation centre and memorial here offer chilling reminders of one of the worst, but little known, atrocities of the war. Every Anzac

Agnes Jones Newton hailed from Illinois and graduated in journalism from the University of California, Berkeley. In 1934, she married Henry G. Keith after meeting him in California while he was on leave from his work in North Borneo. They returned to Sandakan where he was the Conservator of Forests and Director of Agriculture with the North Borneo government. They were imprisoned during the Second World War but survived and returned to Sandakan to help with the post-war rebuilding. Her books documented the periods before, during and after the Japanese occupation.

Day (25 April) a remembrance service is conducted here. There is another memorial in Ranau, where the march ended with just six survivors (five Australians and one British soldier).

Sepilok Orangutan Rehabilitation Centre (see pp. 34–35) is 23km (14 miles) west of Sandakan along Labuk Road, which is the main road out of Sandakan back to Kota Kinabalu via Kinabalu Park. The centre was established in 1964 to rehabilitate once captive or orphaned Orangutans, and viewing platforms provide great vantage points for observing and photographing the animals in a natural setting.

Sepilok is situated next to the Kabili-Sepilok Forest Reserve, which supports lowland forest covering an area of 6,000ha (14,826 acres). The Sun Bear Rehabilitation Centre within the reserve houses some 30 rehabilitated Sun Bears rescued from being illegally kept as pets. The surrounding forest also supports large densities of Red Langurs and Western Tarsiers.

Being some distance from the city centre, joining an organized tour to visit the Sepilok area makes sense, especially for those with limited time. Buses and taxis offer an alternative for independent travellers. Sepilok is open daily from 9 a.m. to noon and 2 p.m. to 4 p.m., with feeding times being at 10 a.m. and 3 p.m. There is a souvenir shop, restaurant, education centre and interpretative display. Various accommodation options, from four-star resorts to hostels, are available just outside the reserve.

The nearby Rainforest Discovery Centre in the Forestry Research Centre is worth visiting to gain a better understanding of Malaysia's complex rainforests. There is an informative display and a short, self-guided nature trail through the adjoining forests. Sighting animals is often difficult

Enjoy traditional English specialties and Asian favourites at Sandakan's English Tea House.

in the rainforest because many species are small and camouflaged, but the canopy walkway provides the opportunity to get a closer look. It is a good location in which to look for Red and Black Giant Squirrels, especially at dusk.

Sepilok's forests are home to numerous bird species, especially those of the Bornean lowland forest. Many birds are most active at dawn and dusk, so unless you can organize your visit at similar times, do not be too disappointed if you just see distant movement. Keen birdwatchers from around the globe flock to Borneo to get a glimpse of Borneo's 61 endemic species. The annual Borneo Bird Festival is staged here in September, and this is one of the best times to visit as extra activities are organized. Look for eight species of hornbill (see p. 82), Bornean Bristleheads, Giant Pittas, trogons, kingfishers, flowerpeckers, spiderhunters and Great Slaty Woodpeckers.

Labuk Bay Proboscis Centre, one-hour's drive from Sandakan (30 minutes from Sepilok), is privately operated within 162ha (400 acres) of coastal mangrove forests facing Labuk Bay, and adjoining oil-palm plantations and degraded secondary forest. While there are feeding facilities, Proboscis Monkeys roam freely through the forest and can be seen from covered viewing areas. There are two feeding platforms and four feeding times – platform A (9.30 a.m. and 2.30 p.m.) and platform B (11.30 a.m. and 4.30 p.m.). On-site accommodation will appeal especially to those who want to get extra close to these unusual primates.

Offshore Islands

Sandakan is the departure point for several offshore islands located in the Sulu Sea, including Turtle Islands National Park, Libaran and Lankayan (see pp. 36–37).

Sabah's second largest port also has a lively waterfront with hotels and restaurants.

The Turtle Islands are famous for their hatchery and programme to release turtle hatchlings back to the Sulu Sea. Sabah Parks manage the three small islands located one hour's boat journey north of Sandakan. Overnight visitor numbers are limited to about 30. As dusk arrives, the turtles start landing on the sandy beach to lay their eggs. Rangers lead tourists to observe this happening, then to the hatchery to release the hatchlings. While accommodation on the Turtle Islands is basic, it is comfortable and provides the added bonus of seeing turtles lay their eggs on every night of the year.

There are few beaches in the region with such fine white sands as those on Lankayan

Island. This is one of Malaysia's quietest outposts, with just a few beachfront chalets from which guests can step directly into the turquoise waters where Blacktip Reef Sharks can be seen swimming in the shallows. The diving here is very good with over 20 dive sites including several wrecks, and this is what attracts most visitors. The many dive sites offer a rich variety of corals, rays, eels, turtles, schools of fish and even the occasional Whale Shark.

Lankayan Island is many things to many people with some travelling here for the diving, others on their honeymoon, some to learn to dive (PADI), while others come to nestle into a hammock and do little else but read a book. Located 90 minutes from Sandakan by fast speedboat, this private island is arguably Malaysia's most idyllic island of white sands and clear turquoise waters. Accommodation is limited which ensures that it will never be overrun and besides, it is quite small and only takes 20 minutes to circumnavigate. There is no television and limited Wi-Fi but this doesn't deter those who come for the diving or the opportunity to witness turtles swimming in the water and laying their eggs in the soft sand. One visitor commented: 'as beautiful as the Maldives but more authentic.'

Puu Jih Shih Buddhist Temple has a commanding position overlooking Sandakan.

Getting There

Sandakan is accessible via a 40-minute flight from Kota Kinabalu, or in three hours by a direct flight from Kuala Lumpur in Peninsular Malaysia.

There is only one boat to Lankayan Island and, apart from the peak season from July to September, departures are only on specific days of the week, rather than daily.. Resort guests need to fly into Sandakan for a 10 a.m. boat departure from the small Sandakan Yacht Club situated close to the city centre and about 20 minutes from Sandakan Airport. Because of the early morning departure, some guests may have to spend the night before departure in Sandakan.

The luxury private island resort is best consulted to develop a personalized itinerary that includes transfers, accommodation and activities around Sandakan. The boat transfer to the island takes about two hours depending on the ocean swell and the return journey departs in the early afternoon.

Where to Stay

Four Points by Sheraton Sandakan
(www.fourpointssandakan.com)
Sabah Hotel
(www.sabahhotel.com)
Sandakan Styles Hotel
(www.sandakanstyleshotel.com)
Sepilok Bed and Breakfast
(www.sepilokbednbreakfast.com.my)
Sepilok Jungle Resort
(www.sepilokjungleresort.com)
Sabah Parks
(www.sabahparks.com)
Lankayan Island Dive Resort
(www.sipadan.com)
Labuk Bay Proboscis Monkey Sanctuary
www.proboscis.cc/accommodation

Elevated walkways through the Rainforest Discovery Centre give views of the rainforest canopy.

Kinabatangan River

The Kinabatangan River, at 560km (348 miles) in length, is Sabah's longest river, and the floodplains of its lower reaches are one of Borneo's most species-rich habitats. Its headwaters are the forested hills near Mount Trus Mardi and the Maliau Basin in the mountainous interior of Sabah. It is also a navigable river up until Bukit Garam.

Rich alluvial soil has been deposited across the floodplain for eons, but much of the riverine forest was converted to oil-palm plantations before it was recognized for its wildlife and ecotourism value. Local and international efforts are now being made to create wildlife corridors that reconnect isolated and broken patches of forest. World Land Trust in partnership with Hutan has secured the Keruak Corridor near Sukau that links the Kinabatangan Wildlife Sanctuary with the Keruak Virgin Jungle Reserve to enable mammals to move freely through a large expanse of riverine forest.

The section of the Lower Kinabatangan centred on Sukau is well worth exploring. It offers a variety of landscapes and is within reasonable access, being just three hours' drive from Sandakan.

Saved from the loggers and oil-palm plantations, the Kinabatangan Wildlife Sanctuary of 52,000ha (133,467 acres) incorporates the Menanggol River, where sightings of Proboscis Monkeys, Orangutans, various other primates, crocodiles and other reptiles, and an extensive list of birds may be seen along this tributary of the Kinabatangan.

The land adjoining the river supports

Most wildlife lodges in the Kinabatangan have river access.

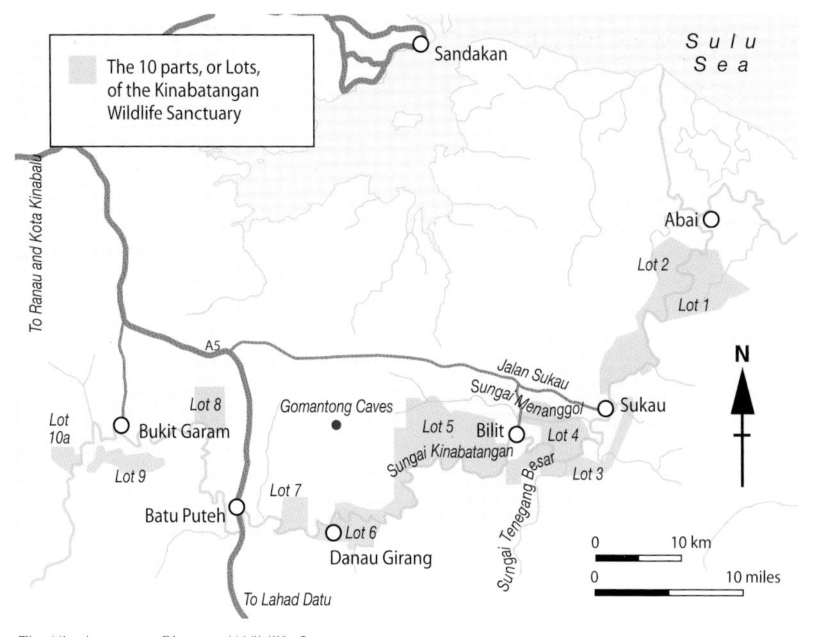

The Kinabatangan River and Wildlife Sanctuary

Malaysia's largest forest-covered floodplain, and most nature tours are focused on cruising along the Menanggol River in small boats, some of which are electric powered.

The brown waters of the Menanggol are some 30m (98ft) wide, and are lined by an overhanging canopy of emergent rainforest trees and lianas. Travelling up the river is like passing through a tunnel deep within the forest. The wildlife concentration here is probably one of the highest in Malaysia, with the main attraction being the Proboscis Monkey, which lives in the riverine forest.

While wildlife spotting can be difficult in other forests, the opportunity is better along the Menanggol than in most other areas. The respected *Phillipps' Field Guide to the Mammals of Borneo* notes that:

'The Kinabatangan River hosts an estimated 3,000 Proboscis Monkey, 1,100 Orangutan and 300 Bornean Elephants. The Kinabatangan is the most important wildlife watching site in Borneo, with at least 20 independent lodges catering to bird and mammal watchers.'

From the comfort of small boats, visitors enter the monkeys' habitat and, if lucky, observe them swinging from branch to branch. Found only in Borneo, the Proboscis Monkey is easily identifiable by its distinctive large red nose. The river is also a haven for Crab-eating Monkeys, macaques, gibbons, crocodiles, Civet Cats, otters and an extensive bird list that includes hornbills.

While the Proboscis Monkey can be

seen in other mangrove, peat-swamp and river-estuary habitats in Borneo, there are almost guaranteed sightings in the Kinabatangan. Males are twice the size of females and easily discernible by their massive orange-red noses and white rump patches that extend down the long tail. The females have less pronounced but pointy noses, and grey rumps and tails.

Proboscis Monkeys also have partially webbed feet and are good swimmers although they do not linger around water, probably because crocodiles and Monitor Lizards also live in the same habitat as them. It is not unusual to see them trying to leap across sections of the Menanggol River, which is a preferred roosting area because the river is so narrow and they do not have to swim far should they want to cross it.

Sightings in the Kinabatangan and its tributaries occur in the afternoon as troops of Proboscis Monkeys return to roost among tall riverine trees after foraging further afield during the day. Typical troops or harems of up to 30 individuals are ruled over by an alpha male, which controls the breeding rights until he is replaced by a more dominant younger male. Alpha males are forever active, leaping among the forest and calling out to continually remind others who is in charge of their respective part

Most lodges in the Kinabatangan are not lavish but provide very comfortable accommodation.

of the forest. While the alpha males are protective of their harems, they are not protective of their territories and can often be seen with langurs and macaques.

Proboscis Monkeys feed on seeds (both ripe and unripe) and leaves of many different plants. In doing so, they contribute to seed dispersal of rainforest plants. Termites also form part of their diet.

The 78,000ha (192,742-acre) Kinabatangan-Segama Wetlands is a Ramsar Site (wetland site of international significance) recognized for its abundant birdlife. It is downstream from the Kinabatangan Wildlife Sanctuary at the mouth of the river where it meets the

An alpha male Proboscis Monkey sitting in mangrove forest along the Kinabatangan River.

Sulu Sea. Waterbirds like the Little Egret, Great Egret, Stork-billed and Blue-eared Kingfishers, Storm's Stork and Darter can be seen here.

While it is possible to travel to Sukau in a mini-van from Sandakan, joining a wildlife expedition tour to the Kinabatangan and Gomantong Caves saves a lot of time and benefits from the services of professional nature guides. Side trips to nearby mangrove forests and freshwater oxbow lakes (meandering sections of the main river that have become cut off from the main river over time) are also possible. There are lodges located just outside the sanctuary near Sukau.

Gomantong Caves

Most tours departing Sandakan for the Lower Kinabatangan River stop on the way at Gomantong Caves situated within the 3,297ha (8,147 acres) Gomantong Forest Reserve (Class V1 Virgin Forest). A fee is charged for visiting the caves. These massive limestone caves (there are two – Simud Putih and Simud Hitam) have been known to the local people for a long time because they have collected prized swiflet nests here for centuries.

The edible nests (comprising saliva and feathers) are essential ingredients in various gourmet Chinese dishes such as bird's nest soup. The soup is highly prized because of the rarity of the bird's nest, its flavour, the supposedly high nutritional value of the dried and hardened bird saliva, and, some say, its aphrodisical properties. It is considered one of the most expensive animal products eaten by humans and is definitely considered a status symbol because of its high cost. A popular variation of the soup is prepared from bird's nest, dried red dates and rock salt. The three are cooked together resulting in a glutinous substance best eaten with a spoon.

Harvesting of the swiftlet nets occurs between February and August with traditional implements made from bamboo and rattan. Two types of nest are harvested here, black and white (the latter is more valuable), and the harvesting takes place after the swiftlet eggs have hatched and the chicks can fend for themselves. Long rattan ladders and bamboo poles are skilfully positioned by dextrous climbers deep

On clear nights, millions of bats fly from the caves of Mulu to forage.

Elevated walkways make walking through the caves safe and easy.

within the caves' crevices with only shafts of light to breach the darkness. An elevated walkway provides access across the mounds of bat and bird guano piled deep on the floors of the two caves.

The best times to visit are at either dusk or dawn, when the changeover of swiftlet and bat populations can be seen (at dusk, the bats fly out and the swiftlets fly in). Watching and hearing the columns of bats leaving the caves (the best cave for this is Simud Putih), and the Bat Hawks and Peregrines Falcons diving in to get a meal is exhilarating. However, most tours from Sandakan arrive outside these hours.

Facilities at Gomantong Caves include a visitor's centre, toilets, a canteen and interpretation displays.

Getting There

There is no public transport to the caves and visitors who try to travel here by themselves face a 3-km (1.87-mile) walk from the main road that leads to the village of Sukau in the Kinabatangan. The caves are located 110km (68 miles) from Sandakan and 35km (22 miles) from the village of Kota Kinabatangan.

Where to Stay

Sukau Rainforest Lodge (www.sukau.com)
Proboscis Lodge (www.sdclodges.com)

Sabah's North-east

Lahad Datu is the air gateway for Sabah's north-east, including Tabin Wildlife Reserve and Danum Valley. Most visitors to this part of Sabah fly to Lahad Datu on MASwings, which runs several daily flights from Kota Kinabalu. Visitors mainly transit through the airport. They generally arrive on organized tours, and are met by lodge staff and vehicles for the various reserves.

The town of 30,000 is a service centre and port for the region. Timber was once important here, but now oil-palm and cacao plantations are located in the surrounding district, with palm biodiesel and oleochemical/fatty acid refining being developed.

Lahad Datu holds little interest for tourists and is more a staging centre for those heading off into the various nature areas in the surrounding region. Its 'wild west' atmosphere (despite being in the east of Borneo) does not help encourage tourism nor do the occasional skirmishes involving lawless intruders from the adjoining Sulu and Celebes Seas.

However, for those who stay awhile there are several decent hotels and restaurants in the town. They may also find some descendants of the Cocos Island Malays who relocated here after the Cocos Islands became part of Australia in the 1950s.

Tabin Wildlife Resort has 10 river and 10 hill lodges.

Tabin Wildlife Reserve

Tabin Wildlife Reserve is located a little over one hour north-east of Lahad Datu on the Dent Peninsula. It is one of Sabah's less discovered natural reserves. It was declared a wildlife reserve because of the large number of animal species inhabiting its forest, including several that are highly endangered. With a protected forest area of 120,500ha (297,762 acres), Tabin plays an important role as a dedicated area for the breeding of Sabah's endangered wildlife and protected mammals.

Tabin makes a valuable contribution to protecting the state's biodiversity, and an increasing contribution to nature tourism. The primary and secondary forests of Tabin make it the largest wildlife park in Borneo. Much of it is covered by secondary regrowth forests, the primary forests having been logged more than 50 years ago. These forests are somewhat open, allowing more sunlight to penetrate the understorey than is the case in primary forests, so spotting wildlife, especially birds, is easier.

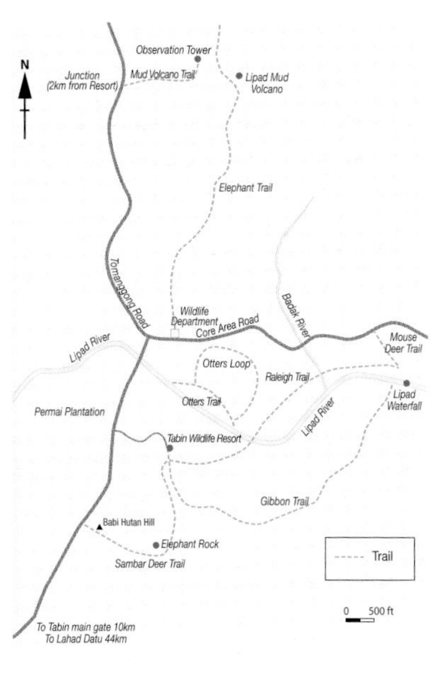

Tabin Wildlife Resoerve.

The secondary forest and primary inner core is home to many birds and other animals. Activities in the reserve include day and night walks, visiting Lipad Waterfall and exploring several streams.

The three largest mammals of Sabah, namely the Bornean Pygmy Elephant, Sumatran Rhinoceros and Banteng, are all thought to be found within Tabin. So rare is the rhinoceros that no one working in the park has recently seen this highly endangered species, but 25 are thought to live here and the occasional hoof marks are sighted. Tabin is the last remaining refuge for the Sumatran Rhinoceros in Borneo.

Some 70 other mammals have been recorded here, and one of the best ways to see them is to join in an organized spotlight night safari on the back of one of the resort's open-roofed vehicles. Orangutans, various deer, Bearded Pigs, Red-leaf Monkeys, Pig-tailed and Long-tailed Macaques, Civet Cats and Silvered Langurs are some of the animals that may be sighted. However, large mammals are virtually impossible to see, although most visitors will be able to observe the telltale signs of elephant dung along the roads and trails, so there is a reasonable chance of spotting elephants.

Birdwatchers will have greater success and a very rewarding time sighting some 320 species, such as all the eight hornbills of Borneo (see p. 82), Asian Paradise Flycatchers, Bornean Bristleheads, Dusky Munias, Large-billed Blue Flycatchers and Blue-headed Pittas. Look a little harder and you may find the rare Speckled Piculet, Chestnut-capped Thrush or Thick-bellied Flowerpecker.

Visitors can also visit a mud volcano, an important feature of the forest known as a salt lick, where wild animals come in search of nutrients. There is an adjoining animal-observation tower that is also good for viewing birds. Not all volcanoes are towering land masses rising above the landscape – the mud volcanoes of Tabin are low structures just a few metres in height, from which mud and steam spew from within the Earth's crust. They can cover an area the size of a football field. The mud contains essential minerals and acts as a salt lick for various animals that come here to supplement their diets.

Tabin Wildlife Resort is an impressive retreat with comfort beyond expectation for such a remote location. A 20-room chalet resort is located next to the park headquarters on the banks of a small river called the Lipad. The river chalets have verandahs perched above the river, and its babbling waters create a very pleasant

Borneo Rainforest Lodge.

ambience. The lodge can sleep up to 80 visitors in various rooming combinations. Its Sunbird Cafe serves hearty local and Western dishes, which are usually buffet style.

Danum Valley Conservation Area

Danum Valley is a two-hour drive due west from Lahad Datu along dusty forest trails. The valley has a core of virgin lowland and hill forest (438 km², 169 sq miles) surrounded by some 10,000km² (3,861 sq miles) of protected and productive (logged) forest. The area is important scientifically and almost unique in that before logging started in the 1970s, the forests had no human settlements. Both the Borneo Rainforest Lodge and the Danum Valley Field Centre are located with virgin rainforest beside the river.

The field centre is available to researchers and students who must apply to visit well in advance. It is well-regarded in the rainforest ecology research community thanks to the support it receives from Yayasan Sabah (Sabah Foundation), the Royal Society and local universities. Researchers have access to plots of both virgin rainforest and logged rainforest for them to make valuable comparative studies.

The canopy walk associated with the Borneo Rainforest Lodge provides one of Asia's best locations for sighting forest birds. Observant visitors could see all eight hornbill species here (see p. 82) as well as gibbons (they might hear the gibbons 'booming' before they see them). Other mammal species to look for in Danum Valley include Orangutans and Clouded Leopards.

The Danum Valley Field Centre is one of the accommodation options. Independent travellers can make arrangements to visit here, and there is a park shuttle van on a few days of the week. The accommodation is comfortable, with cooking facilities for preparing meals.

The Borneo Rainforest Lodge is the other option, albeit a more expensive one. Its guests can discover the magnificent rainforests of Sabah in quite a degree of comfort. Lodge facilities satisfy the needs of international travellers despite their remote location. The dining area and bar overlook the cool, pebble-lined waters of the Danum River. Chalets are constructed from river stones and local timbers, and are modelled on the traditional homes of the local Kadazan-Dusun people. River chalets have private verandahs and soaking tubs, while others are built around tall trees to provide shade.

A team of experienced and enthusiastic guides is employed to ensure that the guests learn as much as they can about the complexities of the rainforest ecosystem. All activities in the rainforest are led by the guides, who pass on their knowledge and identify features that most people may walk past or take for granted.

One of the most popular treks incorporates the canopy walk, a 27-m (89-ft) high traverse through the rainforest canopy. Bird's eye views provide an opportunity to see the forest from a totally new perspective.

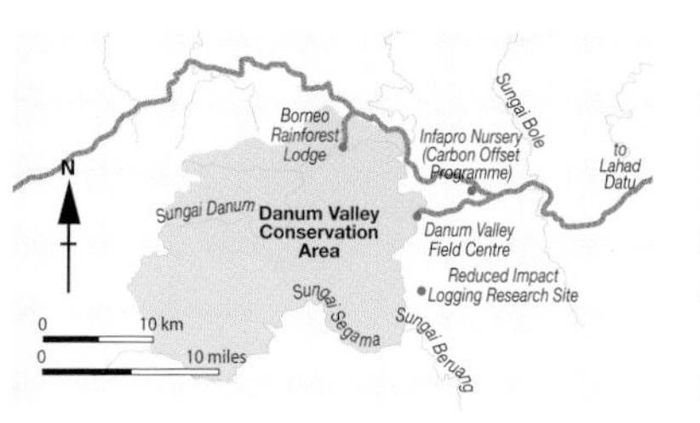

Danum Valley Conservation Area.

Observant and patient visitors will see some wildlife, but time is essential to fully appreciate the animals in this dynamic ecosystem. Literature at the lodge informs visitors that in the forests and rivers around the lodge there are 275 bird species, 110 mammal species (including 10 primates), 56 amphibians and 37 fish, but the list is growing.

The rarest animals in the surrounding forest are the endangered Sumatran Rhinoceros, Clouded Leopard and Bulwar's Pheasant. Others include the Orangutan, Sun Bear, Proboscis Monkey, Elephant, Civet Cat and Flying Squirrel.

At dusk the evening chorus commences with the collective drone of thousands of Emperor Cicadas. As darkness engulfs the valley, fireflies start their synchronous flicker, and pre-dinner drinks take on a completely new dimension as the forest reveals its nocturnal best.

Following dinner, night excursions are offered to witness the nocturnal activities of the animals. These animals are best spotted by looking for their eyes as they are illuminated in the rays of a spotlight.

For a remote rainforest experience, it is hard to go past this lodge. Situated on the

A family of Long-tailed Macaques.

tranquil Danum River, this is definitely the place to commune in Sabah's most pristine lowland and hill forest. The lodge is located 83km (52 miles) south-west of Lahad Datu.

Common Birds of Danum Valley
Argus Pheasant
Borneo Ground-cuckoo
Bristlehead
Crested Fireback
Hornbills (all eight species)
Pitta

Borneo's Hornbill Species
Asian Black Hornbill
Bushy-crested Hornbill
Helmeted Hornbill
Oriental Pied Hornbill
Rhinoceros Hornbill
White-crowned Hornbill
Wreathed Hornbill
Wrinkled Hornbill

Despite its remote location, facilities at the resort are first class.

Getting There

The nearest town to Danum Valley is Lahad Datu. There are daily flights to and from Kota Kinabalu on MASwings. All guest transfers must be arranged by the Borneo Rainforest Lodge. This transfer is part of the full board package that guests pay that also includes accommodation, all meals and guiding services on the nature trails. The road journey of almost 100 km (62 miles) and mostly on gravel roads, takes about two hours from the airport.

Visitors can bathe in the Danum River.

Where to Stay

Tabin Lodge (www.tabinlodge.com)
Tabin Wildlife Resort
(www.tabinwildlife.com.my)
Danum Valley Field Centre
(www.danumvalley.info)
Borneo Rainforest Lodge
(www.borneonaturetours.com)

Sabah's South-east

Sabah's south-east coast includes the towns of Tawau and Semporna, and the offshore dive islands of Sipadan, Mabul, Kapalai and Mataking (see pp. 36–37). Tawau is also the main gateway for Tawau Hills Park north of the town, and the wilderness area of the Maliau Basin Conservation Area in the far southern central region. The south-east faces the Celebes Sea and adjoins North Kalimantan in neighbouring Indonesia.

Tawau

Tawau is the economic centre, with a population of 114,000, and is the service centre for the surrounding district, where timber, cacao, oil-palm and prawn farming are the main economic activities. Tawau Hills Park is just 30 minutes' drive from Tawau, with its highest point being at 1,310m (4,298ft); it supports mossy forest and lowland dipterocarp forest. There is a good trail system, and lodge and dormitory accommodation. Two volcanic areas have been identified beneath the waters of the park's white sulphurous springs, as well as the ancient crater of Mount Lucia. Both are within a few hours' walk from Bombalai Hill volcano near the border with Kalimantan. This is considered to be Malaysia's only substantive volcano, and is thought to have last erupted several thousand years ago.

Semporna

Semporna lies 106km (66 miles) to the east of Tawau, and is the departure point for offshore islands such as Sipadan, 26km (16 miles) to the south-east. Many people here are Bajau, who live in stilt houses over the water on the outskirts of Semporna. Others are Bajau Laut – nomadic 'Sea Gypsies' who live on boats on the clear waters of the Celebes Sea. The Bajau Laut have lived on boats for many years, and the ocean is still their main source of living where they fish and collect clams and mussels. Some are stateless Filipinos who have escaped various conflicts in Mindanao.

The stilt houses of the Bajau Laut off Semporna.

Maliau Basin

Sabah's 'Lost World' wilderness is a large depression enclosed by a high mountain rim and located in the remote far south of Sabah. The basin supports pristine hill forest that is drained by the Maliau River, which joins the Kuamat River before it flows into the Kinabatangan and ultimately the Sulu Sea east of Sandakan.

Tawau provides the best access, but it is still a four-hour drive just to the Maliau Basin Study Centre, then day-long walks to reach the four rudimentary camping sites of Agathis, Belian, Ginseng and Nepenthes. The going is tough and involves very steep climbs, so is best organized by professional trekking companies. However, it is the remoteness that makes the journey so rewarding for those who venture this way, and for the scientists based at the study centre conducting forest research. One of the highlights is Maliau Falls, a multi-step cascade flowing through a gorge that exits the basin. Other activities in the area include a suspension canopy walk, jungle trekking, night safari drives and exploring different forest communities, including heath or *kerangas* forest.

The seven-tiered Maliau Falls.

Getting There

There are direct flights from Tawau to Kota Kinabalu and Kuala Lumpur, plus Tarakan in North Kalimantan. Daily ferries also operate between Tawau and Tarakan.

Where to Stay

Sabah Parks
www.sabahparks.com

SARAWAK

Sarawak is Malaysia's largest and richest state, with substantial resources of oil, gas, timber and palm oil. Though the state's protected national parks and reserves are smaller than elsewhere on Borneo, many natural and cultural adventures await in the 'Land of the Hornbills' for those prepared to venture upriver to the interior and to rough it a little.

Sunset from Damai Beach.

Introduction to Sarawak

Sarawak has a population of 2.64 million people, almost half of whom live along the coast in the three main cities of the capital Kuching, plus Miri and Sibu. Sarawak has the lowest population density of all the Malaysian states, and there are still many isolated tribal communities living upriver in forested settings.

Logging and agricultural development has resulted in large areas of the primary forests being cleared, but there are still many national parks to visit to see wildlife. Some of these are close to built-up areas, so visitors with limited time can still enjoy a variety of natural encounters.

Sarawak's most accessible parks and reserves are around Kuching (Bako National Park, Semenggoh Nature Reserve, Matang Wildlife Centre and Kuching Wetlands), Miri (Lambir Hills National Park) and Bintulu (Similajau National Park). Mulu is also quite accessible as there are direct flights from Miri to the national park. Other popular destinations for ecotourists are Batang Ai, the Kelabit Highlands, Niah Caves and Gunung Gading National Park.

While Sarawak's natural history fascinates visitors, its culture is just as impressive, with more than 30 ethnic tribes or communities living in the state. The main groups are Iban, Malay, Chinese, Bidayuh, Melanau and Orang Ulu. The Sarawak Cultural Village at Damai on the outskirts of Kuching is a showcase of these communities. The village is also the venue for the internationally acclaimed Rainforest World Music Festival (see p. 96).

History

Sarawak has a fascinating history, with the first evidence of humans having been unearthed in the Niah Caves (see pp. 108–109) and dating back 40,000 years. Its more recent history is equally colourful, with Englishman and swashbuckling

Visit Sarawak Cultural Village to experience the state's diverse culture.

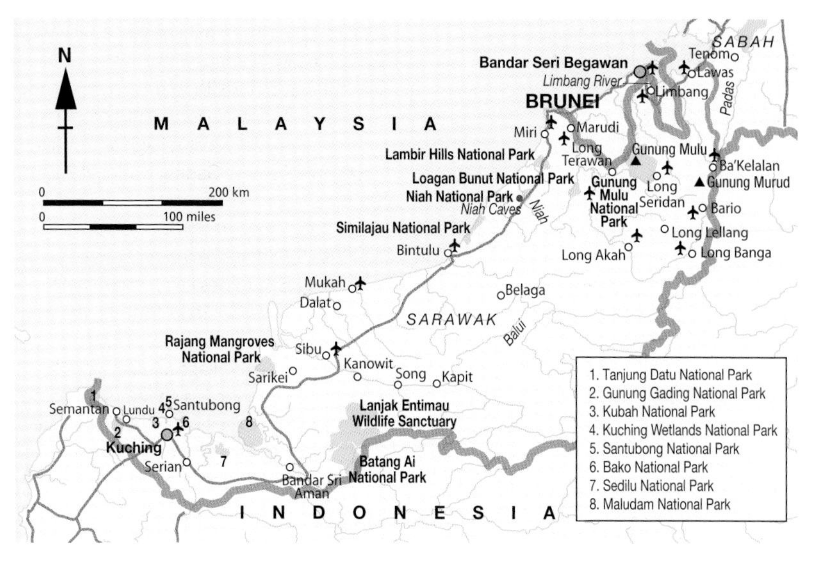

adventurer James Brooke being ceded much of the state by the Sultan of Brunei in 1842 after he suppressed a local uprising (see pp. 14 and 90). He became the first Rajah of Sarawak and ruled until his death in 1868. He was also the first of the 'White Rajahs', who ruled over Sarawak until 1946.

Getting There

While there is a good network of roads in parts of the state, they are mostly confined to the coastal lowlands, with the road from Kuching to Miri being almost 1,000km (620 miles) in length. Many people choose to fly, and tourists should consider doing so to save time. Kuching and Miri are the aviation hubs, with numerous small locations such as Bario, Long Seridan, Long Lellang, Long Banga and Long Akah being serviced by MASwings, which uses 19-seater Twin Otter aircraft. These have limited luggage space so travellers planning on flying to remote destinations need to check the permitted luggage allowances. More adventurous ways of accessing the interior are via riverboats (often small dugouts), or four-wheel drive journeys of discovery. Popular destinations such as Batang Ai are accessed via mini vans, then boats across the lake.

Air circulates around traditional houses built on stilts to keep them cool.

Kuching – Cat City

Kuching is the capital, main air gateway and largest city in Sarawak. While there are several theories about the city's unusual name, one is that it comes from *kucing*, the Bahasa word for cat. The city has capitalized on this idea with cat statues and a Cat Museum. With a population of 325,000, Kuching offers the sophistication of a large city, but with rural areas and beaches less than an hour's drive away. The city centre straddles either bank of the chocolate-brown coloured Sarawak River on which river cruises are popular. This river starts in the foothills to the south of the city and snakes its way for 120km (75 miles) across its floodplain to enter the South China Sea to the south of Bako National Park. Most tourist attractions and commercial activities are on the river's southern bank, while the northern side is more a village though with a few impressive buildings, including the seat of government.

The capital's history adds to Borneo's frontier image, as it was once administered by the White Rajahs (see p. 15). The Brooke Family made Kuching the capital and remained in power for over a century (Kuching was occupied by Japanese armed forces and administrators from 1942 to

Kuching's Chinatown is located close to the popular Waterfront precinct.

1945) and in 1946 the last White Rajah ceded the state as a British Crown Colony.

There is a monument to the Brooke era in front of the Old Court House along Jalan Main Bazaar. The building was the administrative centre for the White Rajahs and the Sarawak Government until 1973. It is now a popular gallery, restaurant, shop and entertainment complex.

Much of the downtown area is flat, so Kuching is an easy city for walking around. Mount Serapi (911m/2,989ft) looms on the horizon to the west of the city.

Some of the most interesting parts of the city to explore on foot are the downtown areas dominated by Chinese shop lots, restaurants and coffeeshops. While Kuching is a multicultural city, it has a substantial Chinese community with those having a Hokkien heritage living in the city precincts and those of Hakka origins mostly living in suburban areas. Other Chinese people in the city have Foochow, Teochew, Cantonese and Hainanese heritage.

Early Chinese settlers arrived by boat via the Sarawak River so it is probably not surprising that they established businesses close to the river. The dominant Chinese parts of the city centre are along Main Bazaar and Carpenter Street close to the river plus,Padungan Road, a little to the west of the city centre.

An interesting circular walk of discovery (one to two hours) is to start from the Old Court House and head in an easterly direction along the Main Bazaar to Tua Pek Kong Temple located at the Temple Street intersection. Turn southward and walk for a short distance before turning westward along Carpenter Street. Walk all the way along this street and beneath the ceremonial gates to Chinatown before returning to the starting point.

The Old Court House in Kuching is now a smart restaurant.

Sarawak Museums

The Sarawak Museum Old Building dates back to 1891 and is Victorian in style with an extension added in 1911. It has one of the region's best ethnography collections. This is well supported by displays of natural history and Sarawak's oil industry. The exhibition of traditional wood carvings is impressive, and there are even stuffed animals dating back to Alfred Russel Wallace's (see pp. 6 and 104) expedition to the Malay Archipelago in the 1850s.

There is a life-sized replica of the interior of a longhouse, and while some exhibits need to be revitalized, the photographs of the many tribes in Borneo provide excellent historical references. Weapons, and body-piercing and tattooing instruments are among the intriguing items.

The galleries at the entrance to the main building are the most current, and extensions under the Sarawak Museum Campus Project are well underway. A royal ceremonial burial trunk on a raised ironwood pole stands at the entrance. Tribal tradition led to exhumed bones of the deceased being displayed in carved trunks placed on high.

There are various other museums in Kuching on Chinese and Islamic history, textiles, petroleum and art, as well as a cat museum (see p. 95). Entry to most is free.

The carved ceremonial burial trunks near the entrance to the Sarawak Museum.

Satok Market

The extensive weekend markets are worth exploring, with their 'wet' (meat and fish) and 'dry' (most other goods) areas. In 2013 the markets were relocated from Satok to their new site, called Medan Niaga Satok, just out of the town in Kubah Ria on the northern banks of the river.

Satok Market is mostly a fresh produce market with an extensive range of fruits, vegetables, meat and fish, as well as food stalls. While much of the produce is recognizable, Borneo is renowned for its variety and the markets do not disappoint, with their red bananas, *dabai* ('tropical olive'), *salak* (snake fruit), durian and edible jungle products like ferns.

Most of the markets are covered, trading starts on Saturday afternoon and continues through to Sunday evening. There are other markets in Kuching, including Jalan Gambier Market near the Brooke Monument. Jalan Gambier is named after a shrub that produces an extract used to dye and tan leather. Gambier was once Sarawak's main export. There is a passageway through to Jalan India, which includes traders and an Indian mosque.

Waterfront

Kuching is rated as one of Malaysia's cleanest cities, and the best place to appreciate this is at the waterfront on the city (southern) side of Sarawak River. This tree-lined promenade is popular with locals and tourists who come here for recreation, to dine in restaurants and to visit a few attractions along the Main Bazaar that runs parallel to the river.

Visitors can take a leisurely stroll to explore the historic buildings, admire modern sculptures and enjoy the fountain. Main Bazaar facing the waterfront is lined with shophouses (former *godowns* or warehouses) selling souvenirs ranging from collectors' items to brassware, pottery, ceramics, tribal arts, wood carvings, masks, blowpipes and shields. Interesting products include Sarawak pepper and edible bird's nests (a Chinese delicacy), and there are also tattoo artists at work

Significant buildings along the waterfront include Square Tower, which was planned as a prison but ended up as a fort. The Chinese Heritage Museum showcases the contributions the Chinese have made and continue to make to Sarawak.

Immediately opposite is the ornately decorated Tua Pek Kong Temple, dating back to 1843. Heading off from here is Jalan Carpenter, lined with old terraces that house commercial activity on the ground floor and residences above. Ceremonial Chinese gates are located at the western end of the street.

Across the River

While the Golden Anniversary Bridge (better known as the 'Golden S' bridge), opened in 2017, over Sarawak River makes the river's northern side more accessible, traditional small *sampans* still make the crossing. Most depart from the waterfront in front of the Hilton Hotel. There are a few stately buildings to visit, and a half-day bike tour around the Malay kampung provides a way of discovering these.

The Astana was built by Charles Brooke and remains as the Sarawak Governor's residence. Nearby, the original Fort Margherita was erected by James Brooke, but the fort on the site is a newer one now housing the Police Museum. The newest structure is the State Legislative Building (also known as the DUN Building), with its references to Bidayuh longhouse architecture. Several day trips from

New bridge across Sarawak River Kuching.

Kuching are possible and many visitors head to Damai Beach, Santubong National Park, Kuching Wetlands National Park and Sarawak Cultural Centre (see pp. 96–97), Semenggoh Nature Reserve (see pp. 34–35) and Bako National Park (see pp. 40–41).

Damai's beaches are quite pleasant and a few resorts here provide a relaxing setting at the base of Mount Santubong (810m/2,700ft). Damai is a great location to relax in after exploring the wilds of Sarawak. Places to discover and activities to engage in include dolphin cruises along the Santubong River, a round of golf at Damai Golf and Country Club, and scaling Mount Santubong.

Being mobile is important as public transport to most of these destinations is limited. City tours only take in the attractions near the centre but tour agents can arrange transfers or visits to most sites outside the town.

To the south of Kuching, Semenggoh Nature Reserve enables visitors to get close to wild and orphaned Orangutans, which are being trained by park wardens to be returned to the wild. Half-day tours are available from the town centre.

Kayaking on the headwaters of the Sarawak River is also possible in the same part of outer Kuching. While this involves a paddle of more than 10km (6 miles), no experience is necessary.

Visitors can gain access to estuarine areas in small boats.

Kuching Wetlands is a Ramsar Site and important as a birdwatching area.

Cat Museum

The small Cat Museum (Muzium Kucing), situated in suburban Petra Jaya, will especially appeal to feline fanciers. Opened in 1993, it has information not only on domestic cats, but also on the native cats of Borneo. An elevated view of Kuching is possible from the front entrance to what is the Kuching North City Hall. For some visitors to Kuching, going to the museum will be a must but for non-cat fanciers, the journey of several kilometres northwards from the city centre, may not hold that much fascination.

The late global traveller and food aficionado, Anthony Bourdain, visited Kuching twice where he ate at Choon Hui Kopitiam and declared the state's famous *laksa* here the 'breakfast of the Gods'.

Day Trips Around Kuching

Annah Rais Longhouse
Bako National Park
Damai Beach
Gunung Gading National Park
Kubah National Park
Kuching Wetlands
Matang Wildlife Centre
Santubong National Park
Sarawak Cultural Village
Sarawak Jong's Crocodile Farm
Satong Island (to see turtles)
Semenggoh Nature Reserve
Matang Wildlife Reserve

Getting There

Many travellers fly to Kuching to discover the city before exploring Sarawak. While government officials work tirelessly to expand air services, the only international flights to Kuching are from Singapore, Brunei and Indonesia (Pontianak). Kuching is tourist friendly, with both international hotels and many local ones, as well as good dining and shopping facilities, plus tourism infrastructure. Like Sabah, Sarawak maintains its own customs and immigration facilities that visitors, even those from Peninsular Malaysia, have to complete.

Where to Stay

Pullman Kuching (www.pullman.com)
Hilton Kuching (www.hilton.com)
Damai Beach Resort
(www.damaibeachresort.com)
Permai Rainforest Resort
(www.permairainforest.com)
Sarawak National Parks
(www.ebooking.sarawak.gov.my)
Hotel Batik Boutique
(www.batik-boutique.hotelsinsarawak.com)
The Ranee Boutique Suites Sarawak
(www.theranee.com)

Coastal Kuching

Due north and one-hour's drive from Kuching are the coastal attractions at Damai and Santubong. Bako National Park is a similar distance to the north-east. Beachside resorts make Damai a pleasant place for a few days' rest and recreation (see p. 95), and the Sarawak Cultural Village is a venue in which to learn about Sarawak's varied and complex cultures. It is also the location for the annual Rainforest World Music Festival (RWMF), normally staged in July.

Damai Beach and mountains.

Key Wetland Species
Proboscis Monkey
Long-tailed Macaque
Silvered Langur
Lesser Adjutant
Saltwater Crocodile
Irrawaddy Dolphin

The Sarawak Cultural Village is a living museum at the foot of Mount Santubong, including a lake and covering 7ha (17 acres). It features six of the 23 cultures represented in the state – the Orang Ulu, Melanau, Iban, Bidayuh, Chinese and Malay people. The traditional homes and lifestyles of these people are showcased, and villagers put on displays to demonstrate their various ways of life. There is a restaurant, auditorium and gift shop.

The three-day RWMF is ranked by *Songlines Magazine* as one of the world's best world music festivals, which welcomes leading international artistes as well as showcasing local musicians. Workshops and a warm, friendly atmosphere make for an enlightening musical experience.

The 6,355m (20,850ft) par 72 Damai Golf and Country Club course has been described by its designer, Arnold Palmer, as: 'the finest test of golf with the most dramatic setting of all in Malaysia. This is a "must play" course for those who love golf.' It is indeed a very picturesque and challenging 18-hole course, with fairways running beside the South China Sea, near mangrove-lined streams and up into the foothills of Mount Santubong.

For walkers, there is a trail to the summit of Mount Santubong. It is best attempted those with experience, as it is at least a six-hour return walk with several very steep and treacherous stretches.

Mount Santubong seen from Sarawak Cultural Village.

Kuching Wetlands

Kuching Wetlands National Park of 6,610ha (16,334 acres), administered by the Sarawak Forestry Department, is Sarawak's only Ramsar Site. Sibu Laut and Salak Rivers flow through it, and mangrove species such as the Loop-root Mangrove thrive here providing a valuable spawning ground for fish and crustaceans.

Nearby, cruises are available on the Santubong River to see Irrawaddy Dolphins and Saltwater Crocodiles. The dolphins do not breach the water, but their dorsal fins are normally sighted during a river cruise.

West of Kuching

Head westwards out of Kuching to Tanjung Datu and the westernmost tip of Sarawak to explore national parks such as Kubah, Gunung Gading and Tanjung Datu, as well as remote beaches and offshore islands.

Kubah National Park

The park of 2,230ha (5,510 acres) was established in 1989 and now incorporates Matang Family Park and Matang Wildlife Centre, where there is an Orangutan rehabilitation programme. The park is especially noted for some 90 palm species that have been identified here; some are found nowhere else in the world. Being so close to Kuching, it is a popular weekend destination for picnics, and its five walking trails are well used. There is a trail to the highest peak and one to a waterfall.

The park is 24km (15 miles) west of Kuching, near the base of Mount Serapi, which is clearly visible from Kuching. Matang, another 11km (6.8 miles) from the park headquarters, is a place to see Orangutans and other animals in reasonably natural surroundings. Accommodation is available in the park.

Long-tailed Macaques are commonly seen in natural areas.

Gunung Gading National Park

This national park is situated further west, near Lundu town, located inland on the meandering Stamin River. Covering 4,106ha (10,146 acres), the park is in a mountainous region of Sarawak and is covered in mixed hill dipterocarp forest. Gunung Gading at 906m (2,972ft) is the highest peak, and several streams flow from the high land. Waterfalls are popular recreational areas and there are several trails, including a two-day return trek to Fortress Rock. Princesses Falls is a pleasant two-hour return jungle walk.

The park is also a place to see the giant rafflesia flower (*Rafflesia tuan-mudae* species, which is only found in the south-west of Borneo) should the plant be in bloom. Joining a ranger-guided tour offers the best chance of locating one. It is best to contact staff in the park to enquire whether the flowers are in bloom before heading here. Hostel and chalet accommodation is available at the park headquarters (designed using traditional Bidayuh roundhouse architecture), and there are some pleasant beachside chalets at Siar and Pandan Lundu just north of Lundu.

The Mousedeer is the smallest known hoofed mammal.

Tanjung Datu National Park

This national park is quite remote and on the way to nowhere. As a result is less visited than others. Access is via a 40-minute boat ride from Semantan or Telok Melano (15 minutes), and is best only attempted when the seas are calm between April and September. Semantan itself is a two-and-a-half-hour drive from Kuching. The park supports mixed virgin dipterocarp forest, beautiful beaches, crystal-clear waters and offshore coral reefs.

Animals such as the Long-tailed Macaque, Silvered Langur, Bearded Pig, Mousedeer and Civet Cat live in the forests, while Green and Olive Ridley Turtles lay eggs on the beach. As turtle eggs are devoured by Monitor Lizards, a ranger-managed hatchery is in place.

Where to Stay

Siar Beach Resort
(www.siarbeachresort.com)
Pandan GoldCoast Holiday Villa
(www.pandangoldcoast.com)
Semantan Palm Beach Resort
(spbresort.com)

The Palmetum is the showcase trail in Kubah National Park.

Batang Ai – Land of Legends

The Batang Ai hydroelectricity scheme and dam project commenced back in 1982, and 24,000ha (59,305 acres) of the surrounding forests were gazetted as Batang Ai National Park in 1991. The lake covers an area of 84km^2 (32 sq miles), although this varies depending on the season. It is well stocked with fish, which are a valuable source of protein for the longhouse communities that live around the shores of the lake.

The park supports primary lowland and hill forest, and its northern border is contiguous with Lanjak Entimau Wildlife Sanctuary (192,800ha/476,419 acres) and Bentung Kerihun in neighbouring West Kalimantan.

Batang Ai is home to Orangutans and

Batang Ai is part of the region's largest protected area.

gibbons, as well as hornbills and many other birds such as the Great Argus Pheasant, Crimson-headed Partridge, White-rumped Sharma and Brown-backed Flowerpecker.

Iban Hospitality

Some Iban longhouse communities welcome visitors and have installed special facilities to accommodate homestays. These can be an hour's boat journey from civilization, and access is by small dugout boats powered by outboard motors.

Despite the hydroelectric dam, some upriver longhouses are dependent on diesel generators for their electricity supply. Longhouses like Ng Mengkak Ulu Engkari are remote and do not have mobile phone reception or Wi-Fi.

The community of 27 doors and some 150 residents is housed under an elongated rusty tin roof built high above the lake. The number of doors in Iban society equates to the number of families in the community. Entry to the longhouse is normally via a bathing place along a river (or in the case of the dam, the foreshore), which is a symbolic representation of the community's outer threshold. The suggestion is that visitors bathe before being welcomed into the longhouse community.

Long, open communal verandahs are where all the community activities are conducted. Family life, including cooking and sleeping, occurs behind closed doors along the rear of the verandah. Storage space for personal belongings is available in the form of a loft located above each family room. During the heat of the day most of the villagers return from tending their fields and rest, before returning to work in the cool of the late afternoon.

Many of those on the verandah during work hours are the old and the young, but school-age children spend the week at boarding school, returning to the longhouse at the weekend. Society is changing in many longhouses as older teenagers move to the cities for education and employment.

Trails and streams become one in some parts of the national park.

Visitors are made to feel that they are guests rather than tourists. In some longhouses women may still weave the intricate local *pua kumba* cotton cloth, but this too is becoming a lost craft. The walls of the longhouse are lined with various instruments, baskets, mats and even the occasional blowpipe. While some villagers maintain their skills with blowpipes to kill animals, others use guns.

Most longhouses are located close to a river or the lake foreshore around Batang Ai.

Iban hospitality is best experienced at a mealtime, when families gather in their individual areas next to the kitchen. Meals are taken on a mat on the floor and could include local dishes such as *pansoh manok* (bamboo chicken) and *asi pansoh* (rice in bamboo). Tea is served and *tuak* (rice wine) accompanies most meals, especially when guests are around. In the evening, visitors are offered a welcoming glass or two of *tuak* and entertained with dance performances under the light provided by the hum of the generator off in the near distance. Afterwards, mattresses beneath mosquito nets are set up for the evening's rest along the verandah.

Nanga Sumpa Longhouse on the banks of the Delok River is another forest homestay located 90 minutes by boat upriver from the lake.

Resort Longhouse

The Aiman Batang Ai Longhouse Resort on the foreshore of Batang Ai is halfway between an authentic longhouse and a deluxe hotel. It is perched beside the lake and constructed along traditional Iban lines.

Interestingly, the resort rooms do not overlook the lake – in traditional Iban culture, the sleeping quarters are furthest from the side from which the enemy would attack. In the past, enemies would have approached from the water, so the long, open verandahs of each longhouse building at the resort occupy the prime position, and the guestrooms face the gardens. While the view is not as spectacular as vistas of the lake, Iban customs were followed in the building of the resort rooms so as not to offend the spirits that live in the lake.

Unlike many properties, the Aiman resort

openly encourages its guests to leave the confines of the compound. Most of the attractions are in the adjoining jungle, so recreational facilities in the resort are limited – although the pool is a welcome retreat from the tropical weather.

Activities include naturalist-guided walks starting at dawn, rainforest treks, lake cruises, an elevated canopy walk, waterfall excursions, camping and fishing. This is really a resort for getting close to nature.

Batang Ai is 250km (155 miles) or a four-hour drive from Kuching, with most tour companies using a mini-van to the boat jetty, then a 20-minute journey across the dam lake on a small boat. As a whole day is spent travelling there and back, it is wise to spend at least two nights at Batang Ai.

Two of the highlights of the road journey are a stop at the Bidayuh market town of Serian and a visit to a pepper farm, where the best Sarawakian peppercorns can be purchased for a fraction of the price that global gourmands pay for what is considered to be one of the world's best peppers. Pepper was first planted in Sarawak in 1856 and the berries of the pepper vine grow in small grape-like clusters. Some 67,000 rural dwellers grow pepper which thrives in upland areas on fertile hill slopes.

The 'king of spices' or 'black gold' has been grown in Malaysia for many decades but Sarawak's 31,000-tonne (34,172-ton) production now accounts for 98 per cent of the country's total production. Malaysia is the fifth largest exporter of pepper around the world with neighbouring Vietnam holding the top position. Malaysia is known for its high-quality pepper with some 24 per cent being exported to Japan.

Where to Stay

Nanga Sumpa Lodge
(www.borneoadventure.com)
Aiman Batang Ai Longhouse Resort and Retreat
(www.aimanbatangai.com)

Visitors can stay in the relative luxury of the Aiman Batang Ai Longhouse Resort.

Sibu, Mukah and the Rajang River

Sibu is considered a boom town and owes its success and wealth to the logging industry, which peaked a few decades back. It created many millionaires and today the town has a noticeable number of palatial homes. Sibu is also the gateway to coastal towns such as Mukah and upriver destinations along the upper reaches of the Rajang River.

James Brooke settled the area and in 1862 built a fort here for protection. Budding historians and naturalists should enquire about visiting Sarikei, to the south-west of Sibu. It was in James Brooke's cottage at Bung Muan near Bukit Peninjau that noted naturalist Alfred Russel Wallace (see p. 8) conducted some of his important research.

Sibu has a population of 165,000, with much of it being of Chinese descent, although Melanau, Iban and Bidayuh people also live here. Many of the early Chinese settlers were Christians and left China after being persecuted during the Boxer Rebellion of 1889 to 1901. The initial migrants were Hokkien, Hakka, Foochow (Fuzou) and Teochew, who arrived in Sibu in 1901 and became farmers. They became established and successful, and built schools, churches, temples and hospitals. The World Fuzou Heritage Gallery commemorates the hard work done by the early Foochow settlers, while the Sibu Cultural Heritage Museum provides an insight into the diversity of the Sibu people.

Rubber was introduced in 1904 and the community prospered in the early years, but the wealth really started to be generated in the 1970s, when logging became a lucrative industry. Sibu was ideally

Downtown Sibu in central Sarawak has many modern buildings.

located as logs could be floated or barged to it from the upper reaches of the river. Plywood factories, sawmills and shipbuilding developed as part of the logging industry.

Multicultural Sibu is best reflected in its places of worship, with the Tua Pek Kong Temple, Sacred Heart Cathedral, Masland Methodist Church and An-Nur Mosque existing among many others. Yu Lung San Tien En Si (Jade Temple), located on the Sibu to Bintulu Road, caters to devotees of Buddhism, Taoism and Confucianism, and is ranked as one of the largest temples in the region.

Before the area was cleared for agriculture, much of it was covered in peat-swamp forest; Bukit Lama Peat Swamp of 390ha (964 acres) is a remnant patch of this original forest. Located within this is a public-access forest park of 219ha (541 acres), with two extensive boardwalk trails through it.

Sited on Jalan Channel, opposite the express-boat passenger terminal, Sarawak's largest undercover market is not to be missed. Sibu Central Market (Pasar Sentral Sibu) extends over several storeys, and has a large food-stall area on the second floor. This lively venue is a must-visit destination, with a wet and dry section as well as an area devoted to local produce. Some stalls are temporary, with the vendors displaying their produce on mats covering the floor. This is the place to see colourful ginger flowers, juicy melons, squirmy sago worms, multicoloured Sarawak layered cake, organic Bario rice (red, black, brown and white varieties), forest produce such as fresh edible ferns, and handicrafts. One of the most interesting sights is in the poultry section, where chickens and ducks are wrapped and packed in sheets of newspaper awaiting easy transport from the market to someone's home and the cooking pot.

Tua Pek Kong Temple is a famous landmark in Sibu.

Famous Sibu prawn noodles (*mee udang*) are served in several hawkers' stalls located above the general market area.

Mukah

River ferries operate down the Rajang River from Sibu to Dalat. From here, smaller boats provide a connection to Mukah, located at the mouth of the Mukah River. Mukah is a bustling market town with a lively fish market where freshwater fish, as well as fish caught in the South China Sea, are eagerly snapped up by the locals.

Homestay accommodation in a Melanau longhouse is offered in the riverine village of Kampung Tellian.

'Gift-wrapped' chickens in Sibu Market awaiting somebody's cooking pot.

Mangrove and nipa-palm forests lining the smaller watercourses in this area provide valuable materials – from food to building materials – for the locals. There is a thriving sago industry along the banks of the small stream here. Cut sago-palm logs line the stream before being processed to extract the starch and 'pearls' that are used in cooking.

Fishing is also important and ecotourism activities are developing along the small streams lined with forests.

Rajang River

Sibu is situated on the Rajang River, and travellers can choose to go downriver or upriver to participate in various adventurous activities. At 563km (350 miles), the Rajang is Malaysia's longest river, just a bit longer than the Kinabatangan. Sibu is located some 60km (37 miles) from the river mouth and the South China Sea.

The river is tidal for a considerable distance from its mouth, but is navigable by large boats all the way upriver to Kapit, 160km (100 miles) or three hours upstream. The river here is 200m (660ft) wide. However, further upstream various rapids make it impossible for large boats to navigate, and smaller boats are carried across the rapids. Here the Rajang River is joined by the Baleh River, which flows down from the mountainous highlands on the border with West Kalimantan. The Rajang continues past the famous Pelagus Rapids just before Belaga, then to the huge Bakun Dam, the biggest dam in Southeast Asia. This is the heartland of the Kayan and Kenyah people.

The upper reaches of the river are mountainous, and the river has always served the local Orang Ulu residents as the lifeline to the outside world. The river is mostly straight here, but it starts to meander on the flat alluvial floodplain downriver from Sibu.

Local guides can be engaged to provide access to Kayan longhouses or Penan communities. The small town of Song is one such destination, and the starting point for treks to Iban longhouses along the Katibas River. Boats depart from Song and travel up this tributary of the Rajang, but it is best to engage a guide in Song or Sibu before setting off to longhouses such as Nanga Bangit, Nanga Engkuah and Rumah Api.

Kapit is sited more deeply in the interior. Despite its isolation, it too has a fort – Fort Sylvia – built in 1880 by the White Rajahs to defend their territory. The Civic Museum has interesting information and displays on the tribes of the Rajang Valley, and on the lives of the Hokkien traders who were among the earliest settlers in the district. The town is big enough to support banks, hotels, restaurants and cafes.

Getting There

Sibu Airport is the second largest in the state after Kuching. There are direct flights from Kuala Lumpur on Malaysia Airlines and AirAsia. MASwings flies from Sibu to Bintulu, Kota Kinabalu, Kuching, Miri and Mukah. AirAsia also flies to Kuching.

Sibu is connected by road to Kuching (192km/119 miles), but many locals travel by express boat or fly (it takes four hours by express boat). Riverboat services also extend to Belaga, Dalat, Dalat, Daro, Kapit, Kanowit, Sarikei and Song.

Where to Stay

Premier Hotel (www.premierh.com.my)
Tanahmas Hotel (www.tanahmas.com.my)
Lamin Dana Cultural Boutique Lodge (www.lamindana.com)

Small boats provide the fastest transport between villages around Mukah.

Niah Caves

Niah Caves are 110km (68 miles) south of Miri. While the cave fauna is significant, it is their archaeology that makes them so unique. Fragments of human skulls found here, dating back 45,000 years, have provided the region's earliest evidence of *Homo sapiens*. An on-site Archaeological Museum documents this history, with some original and replicated remains on display.

Major Tom Harnett Harrisson was one of those larger-than-life characters who helped shape Sarawak. Born and educated in England, he spent much of his adult life in Sarawak, where he mastered many disciplines, including being an ornithologist, museum curator, military officer, writer and archaeologist. He was often described as a 'barefoot anthropologist' and is best known as being the curator of Sarawak Museum from 1947 to 1966.

The Great Cave was a burial site for at least 166 *Homo sapiens*, but this area is fenced off. Archaeological digs were initiated in 1954 under the watchful eye of Tom Harrisson (and his wife Barbara), and his research hut still stands at the mouth of the cave.

Further along the dark trail is Painted Cave, where the remains of wall paintings stretch along 32m (105ft); they are safely guarded by an iron fence.

Cave Fauna

During the day most of the cave life is resting, so bats and swiftlets are not active.

45,000 year old human remains have been found in Niah Caves.

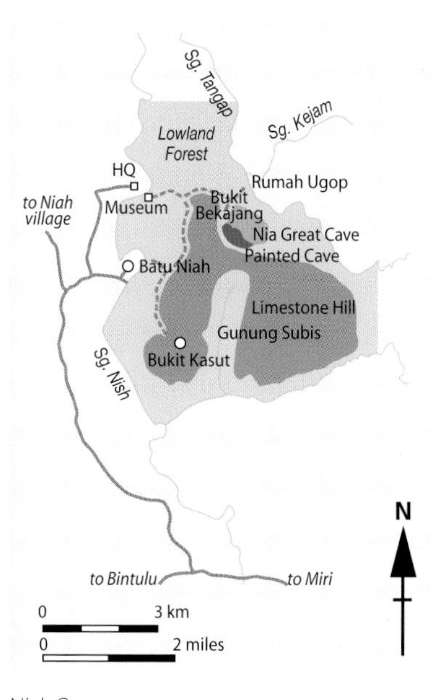

Niah Caves.

Dusk is the best time to see them. These cave dwellers are also very important in the food chain, as swiftlets devour insects and bats pollinate many forest plants – while the fruit bats feed in the forests, they pollinate plants at the same time. The animals roost on the cave ceiling during the day, then stream out at dusk to do their essential activities with the plants. Although this phenomenon is nowhere near as spectacular here as it is at Mulu Caves (see pp. 38–39), swiftlets, bats and raptors can be seen.

Swiftlets build nests high up in the dark recesses of the caves, and there is a complex system of bamboo scaffolding to enable villagers to harvest the nests between August and March. Conservationists are concerned that swiflet and bat numbers have been seriously depleted due to over-harvesting and the conversion of neighbouring forests to oil-palm plantations.

To complete the cave's ecological cycle, the droppings of bats and swiftlets are also harvested for fertilizer.

Getting There

Joining an organized day tour to the 3,138ha (7,754-acre) park is recommended, but intrepid travellers will find that it is possible to use public transport from Miri to reach Batu Niah, then travel on to the park on foot (a 45-minute walk) or a short taxi ride (taxis wait at the bus stop in Batu Niah). There is a small boat crossing of the Niah River into the park; do not try and swim it because there are crocodiles in the river.

Reaching the caves requires a considerable amount of walking (a 10km/6.2-mile return trip), mostly on wooden boardwalks. Wear good shoes, drink plenty of water, use a sunscreen and wear a hat. The walk is not really suitable for young children. Torches are essential for negotiating the dark cave passages; take your own or hire one from the park. There is a cafeteria selling local food, an interpretation cetnre and ranger headquarters.

Where to Stay

Sarawak Forestry provides a selection of acommodation that is quite comfortable considering the relative isolation of the site. Hostel rooms for example, have four single beds, a private bathroom and are cooled by fans. The cafeteria remains open until late in the evening. There is alternative accommodation just outside the park entrance in the small town of Batu Niah. Sarawak National Parks (www.ebooking.sarawak.gov.my)

Miri and the North-east

Miri is the centre of Malaysia's lucrative oil industry. With a population of more than 300,000 people and rising, it is a booming city, but one that still retains distinctive elements of the various local cultures and of the Chinese people who settled here many years ago.

Canada Hill, where the 'Grand Old Lady' is located, is the site of Malaysia's first commercial oil well, spudded in 1910. There is an interactive oil museum here that appeals to children, as well as good views of the city from the museum's verandah.

North-eastern Sarawak is home to many of Sarawak's ethnic communities, including Iban, Malay, Chinese, Melanau, Bisaya, Orang Ulu (mostly Kayan, Kenyah, Kelabit and Lun Bawang), Bidayuh, Indian and Eurasian, as well as a sizeable community of oil workers who come from many parts of the world.

Miri City Sights

While Miri may once have been merely an airport for tourists to transit through en route to destinations such as Mulu Caves, there are now many reasons to spend a few days in this coastal city. In addition to having vibrant a nightlife and being a shopper's delight, Miri has several tourist attractions.

Tamu Muhibbah is the local market, where many fascinating local products from the Sarawakian interior are available for sale. Native jungle produce features in this 24-hour-long market located opposite the Park Hotel. Orang Ulu people travel downriver to sell their produce, and a walk around the market provides an illuminating lesson in jungle nutrition.

Even veteran market goers can find something unusual here, be it a new variety of banana (red, for example), mangoes resembling turnips, famous brown and white rice from Bario, and jungle remedies made from hard-to-find plant and animal byproducts. Colourful characters run impromptu stalls established on rattan mats, selling other products like yellow cucumbers that resemble mangoes, huge crimson durians, tiny sponges and *tuak* (rice wine). There is a large selection of dried and fresh seafood, such as *bubok* (tiny prawns) and big

buckets overflowing with catfish.

The Miri Handicraft or Heritage Centre has been upgraded and features cottage industry products such as baskets, hats, textiles and beadwork jewellery, for which this part of the world is noted. There are over a dozen retail outlets selling products made by Kelabit, Kayan, Lun Bawang, Dayak and Melanau people.

Eastwood Valley Golf and Country Club is just five minutes' drive from the airport. The signature thirteenth hole is the one most golfers enjoy playing. While just a short par 3, its island green design tests most golfers.

Much of the foreshore has been reclaimed, with hotels such as the Pullman Waterfront overlooking the Baong River and the South China Sea, and the Miri Marriott Resort and Spa plus ParkCity Everly located outside the city centre beside the South China Sea. Service boats for the offshore oil industry moor along the Baong River, and there is always lots of activity with boats coming and going.

The colourful San Ching Tian Tao Temple, on the outskirts of Miri, is the largest of its

Some of the best views of coastal Miri are from the Pullman Waterfront Hotel.

The local tamu *or market has a range of exotic fruits and vegetables.*

type in Southeast Asia. Another place for reflection is the tranquil Japanese Gardens located in the city centre.

Alternatively, those yearning for the bright lights can enjoy Miri's party town atmosphere, range of restaurants, lovely pubs and nightspots that especially cater to visitors from neighbouring Brunei.

Festive Miri

Sarawak is becoming the music festival state in Malaysia, hosting the Rainforest World Music Festival in Kuching (see p. 96) and two annual festivals in Miri.

The Borneo Jazz Festival in May is an international festival that was originally staged in the open air beside the Miri beachfront over two tropical nights. More recently, the festival has moved downtown within a five-star hotel near the waterfront. While the musicians set a scintillating beat, the setting and crowd are very relaxed, with a family atmosphere. Country and Western music is also popular in this part of Borneo, and an annual festival staged in February celebrates this music genre.

Four of Malaysia's best known and visited national parks, Gunung Mulu, Lambir Hills, Niah Caves (p. 108) and Loagan Bunut, are all accessible from Miri. It is therefore a gateway for eco-adventures in these parks, as well as to remote communities like Bario and Ba'Kelalan in the far north-east of the state.

Gunung Mulu National Park

Gunung Mulu National Park (see also pp. 40–41) especially appeals because of the massive limestone caves beneath the mostly untouched forests and the jagged mountains above the land. One of the most impressive landforms in the park is the Pinnacles located on Gunung (Mount) Api and Benarat. These razor-sharp limestone spikes rise up to 40m (130ft) above the rainforest. Experienced trekkers intent on a demanding climb need to book in advance for the three-day return walk.

While the landscape was formed millions of years ago, it is slowly but constantly evolving through the erosive forces of water flowing through the caves. At the same time, water enriched with dissolved calcium carbonate slowly drips through cave cracks and crevices, creating more limestone. Stalactites and stalagmites are the obvious signs of such deposition.

These caves are massive and extensive, with Clearwater Cave mapped at 100km (62 miles) in length. The Clearwater River flows through it, and scientists believe it to be one of the world's longest underground rivers.

Lambir Hills National Park

Lambir Hills National Park of 70km² (27 sq miles) is within an easy drive from Miri, and travellers passing through the city can happily spend a few hours here exploring the network of trails.

The park is considered to be Sarawak's most important stand of remaining virgin coastal forest. While hunting has reduced the numbers of large mammals, it has the richest forests in all of Asia after Kinabalu Park. Rainforests have developed on a range of low sandstone hills, and it is this topography and the varied soil types that have resulted in the park's diverse flora. Scientists have noted that the forests are a relic of a much vaster forest that once covered much of the region. Lambir Hills is of major scientific interest because its tree diversity is only exceeded by one other location in the world, Yasuni in Peru. In a 52ha (128-acre) patch of rainforest, 470,000 trees of 1,200 species have been identified by scientists. However, the loss of the park's animal population concerns scientists because many of the seeds from trees are dispersed by animals – without them, there could be a collapse in tree diversity for this globally significant ecological site.

Interesting communities of stunted *kerangas*, or heath forests, are located on elevated ridges. *Nepenthes* pitcher plants are commonly found here.

There are several waterfalls and a tower for a good view over the forest canopy. Some 100 bird species have been recorded in the park, and the viewing towers provide

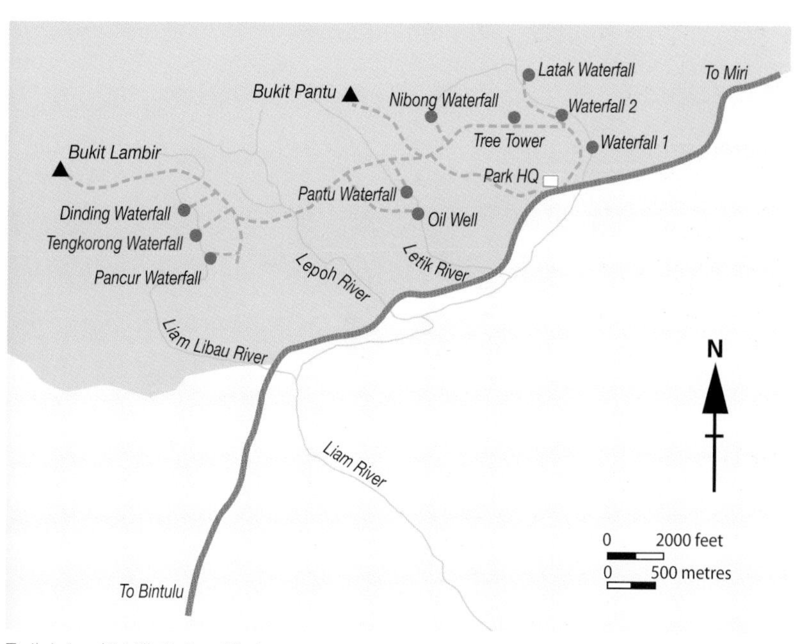

Trails in Lambir Hills National Park.

a sheltered and shaded location for viewing some of them. There are eight waterfall pools for cooling off in the tropical heat.

Simple park accommodation is available for those who want to spend a few days in the park's peaceful solitude. Getting to the park is relatively easy from Miri, and hiring a taxi is the best way of doing so, although buses to Bintulu or Bakong regularly pass the park entrance, located 30km (11.5 miles) south of Miri.

Diving

While oil exploration and diving normally don't coexist, diving in Miri is becoming more developed with some of the sites being located close to some of the oil platforms. Exploring the reefs just offshore is possible with several sites being within a 30-minute boat journey from Miri. Some 28 sites have been identified along a 30-km (19-mile) stretch of the Miri coastline from Lutong in the north to Sibuti in the south.

Miri is the gateway to the dramatic limestone Pinnacles of Mulu.

Here enthusiasts can dive around the best known sites named Eve's Garden, Anemone Garden, Azam's Reef, Tusan, New Reed V, Sea Fan Garden and North Point or around the two shipwrecks including Atagomaru Wreck.

Miri is considered by some dive experts as a rich and untapped resource that few divers know about. It is rich in corals, nudibranchs and fish, and Whale Sharks have also been seen around the shallow waters of these offshore reefs.

One of the big advantages for the diving industry here is that most of the reefs are very close to the city of Miri, which has an abundance of accommodation, restaurants and shops plus a lively nightlife in addition to being well connected by several airlines.

Getting There

AirAsia and Malaysia Airlines have several flights a day from Peninsular Malaysia to Miri, as well as from other destinations in Borneo such as Kuching and Kota Kinabalu.

Miri is also a hub for small aircraft servicing rural destinations around the state. MASwings uses a fleet of ATR and Twin Otter aircraft to provide an essential service to small communities, and to enable travellers to access several remote communities. These include Ba'Kelalan, Bario, Long Akah, Long Banga, Long Lellang and Seridan. It also flies from Mulu to bigger destinations such as Bintulu, Kota Kinabalu, Kuching, Labuan, Limbang, Lawas, Mukah and Sibu. The aircraft, especially the Twin Otter, have limited luggage space, and passengers are restricted in what they can carry (10kg/25lb per passenger).

The Pan-Borneo Highway (called the Trans-Kalimantan Highway in Kalimantan) is an ongoing development project to connect many parts of Borneo. It will be 3,073 km (1,909 miles) in Kalimantan, 2,083 km (1,294 miles) in Malaysia and 168 km (104 miles) in Brunei.

Miri's San Ching Tian Ta Temple.

Where to Stay

Pullman Waterfront (www.pullmanhotels.com)
Miri Marriott (www.marriott.com)
ParkCity Everly (www.theeverlyhotel.com)
Sarawak National Parks (www.ebooking.sarawak.gov.my)

Limbang and Lawas

A thin strip of Sarawak including the town of Limbang divides the nation of Brunei into two parts, separating the main western division from the eastern.. Apart from a small stretch of coastline along the South China Sea, Brunei's eastern division is surrounded by Sarawak, with the town of Lawas located between Brunei and Sabah. These are two small towns of fewer than 40,000 inhabitants each, but they were and remain important regional market towns.

Limbang

The town of Limbang is located on the Limbang River, which provides access for its residents to travel downriver to coastal destinations. Rice and sago produced in the district are traded with Brunei. The town's strategic location captured the attention of Rajah Charles Brooke, who in 1890 annexed the territory for Sarawak from the Sultan of Brunei (see p. 14).

There are few attractions in Limbang apart from the regional museum (formerly a fort built by the White Rajahs), and a farmers' market held every Friday. The town is large enough to warrant comfortable hotels and a shopping centre.

Adventurous travellers can enter the town off the exit from Gunung Mulu National Park (see pp. 38–39) via the Headhunter's Trail, which is a three-day, two-night expedition (it can be shorter) that involves various modes of transport, including boating, trekking and riding in a mini-van. An organized tour with a travel agent includes transportation and guides, and involves overnight accommodation in rangers' quarters and Rumah Bala Lesang, which is an Iban longhouse.

Limbang was originally part of Brunei.

Expect a warm welcome from the locals in these remote parts of Borneo.

Lawas

Unlike with Limbang, Charles Brooke purchased the Lawas District from the Sultan of Brunei. Located a few kilometres inland on the Lawas River, this is quite a bustling town that became wealthy through logging. Market days in the town are liveliest on Friday night through to Saturday afternoon. The market is a good place to buy some upland products such as handicrafts, Ba'Kelalan salt and Bario rice, as well as fresh fruits and vegetables.

Overland travellers from the Kelabit Highlands communities of Ba'Kelalan and Bario can use Lawas as the access point, although the road journey is along rough, dusty former logging roads.

Getting There

Limbang and Lawas both have airports serviced by MASwings with flights from Limbang to Kota Kinabalu, Lawas and Miri, and from Lawas to Ba'Kelalan, Limbang and Miri. There is a road from Limbang through Brunei to Lawas. Ferry boats travel down the Limbang River to the Bruneian capital of Bandar Seri Begawan, and to Lawas and Labuan. Ferries also connect Lawas to Labuan, Brunei and Limbang. Lawas and Limbang hav no road connection with Sarawak, although Lawas is connected to southern Sabah via a road to Tenom.

Where to Stay

Purnama Hotel (www.penviewhotel.com)

Sarawak Interior

There are few places in Borneo as remote as Sarawak's interior and destinations like Bario and Ba'Kelalan. Sarawak's highest mountain, Mount Murud (2,424m/7,946ft), is located just south-west of Ba'Kelalan, while this part of Sarawak borders Kayan Mentarang National Park in Indonesia (see p. 135) and walks are offered to Mount Murud, Kalimantan and to Bario.

Things move slowly in the interior, and only a few decades ago the children of Ba'Kelalan walked for five days to get home from the boarding school they attended in Lawas (six hours' drive away, or about 125km/78 miles). Activities in the region are measured in how many days it takes to walk to various destinations. Considering that much of the surrounding countryside is tropical rainforest with undulating buttress roots along the way and rapidly flowing rivers, the difficulty in moving about is even more significant.

Communities like Bario and Ba'Kelalan have reasonable tourism infrastructure, with the former being popular with backpackers. Most communities here grow the famous upland rice, while Ba'Kelalan is gaining notoriety as Malaysia's only producer of apples.

Many of the communities in the interior are Christian and conservative, and traditional values reign supreme among them.

Rice fields Ba'Kelalan.

Ba'Kelalan

Ba'Kelalan is an isolated Christian community of 1,500 residents, one hour by small plane from Miri. Its Lun Bawan people were once fierce headhunters, but Christian missionaries put a stop to that as well to drinking and smoking.

Walking is something most visitors do here in the relatively cool air at 1,000m (3,280ft) above sea level. Walking to all nine rice-growing communities in the valley takes all day. A good walk can involve heading up the hill opposite the tiny airport to a Sanui Viewpoint to get a comprehensive impression of the landscape. Keen adventurers may want to consider walking to other destinations, such as Krayan (Long Bawan) on the Kalimantan side of the border (4km/2.5 miles), or Bario. Another possibility is an ascent of Mount Murud (with the assistance of local guides).

While the harvesting of Malaysia's only apple orchard is newsworthy enough, the lifestyle and agricultural practices of the community provide other good reasons to visit this peaceful community. The organic apple orchard of 1,000 trees (five varieties) was established from cuttings brought in from Java in 1975. New apple trees have recently been planted and will bear fruit in a few years. While the apple harvest is unique, rice production is essential for sustaining the community. Highland's wet *padi* rice is known as *adan*, commonly called Bario rice, and is highly prized for its fragrance. Irrigation is often used and buffaloes are harnessed to till the soil. The rice is planted in July and harvested in January, and no machinery is used.

Personal greetings are very important in the highlands and most people will stop to talk to visitors. The villagers are happy to demonstrate to visitors their daily routine of growing rice and vegetables, hunting, raising livestock, cooking, producing salt (in Buduk Bui) and making handicrafts. Being so isolated, the residents are resourceful in finding materials in the natural forest and crafting utilitarian items, especially from bamboo. Handicrafts are another part of village life, and the delicate, colourful bamboo products such as baskets make excellent value-for-money souvenirs. Singing, dancing (especially the bamboo dance) and music performed by the women's bamboo pipe orchestra keep visitors entertained.

Ba'Kelalan is also home to one of Malaysia's most remote and least-developed golf courses. With a grand title of Meligan Highland Golf and Country Club, the nine-hole, cow-grass 'fairways' and 'greens' may not be ready for Tiger Woods, but they more than adequately cater to the community's budding golfers. Visitors will find the course to be a curiosity rather than a playable option.

Homestay accommodation is offered in several low-key properties in the village. Electricity in the community is generated by a micro hydroelectric plant and solar power.

Bario

Bario, located in the remote highlands of Sarawak and accessible by flights from Miri, is home to the Kelabit people. It is 1,000m (3,280ft) above sea level, so has a refreshingly cool climate that makes it perfect for walking in the hills. The Kelabit residents were once headhunters, but have now embraced Christianity. However, some older men still have tattoos, while the women wear heavy brass earrings on their elongated earlobes and display intricate beadwork.

Colourful handicrafts made by the Lun Bawang people.

Bario in the Kelabit Highlands is ringed by forested hills, and various tracks make it suitable for extended jungle treks. It is possible to fly into Bario, trek overland for several days staying in longhouses, then fly out of places like Long Lellang.

A popular walk is a pleasant but demanding five-hour (one-way) trek across undulating hills to a longhouse called Pa'Lungun, where comfortable and reasonably priced guesthouse accommodation is available. Trekkers follow the old buffalo trail and pass through the hamlet of Pa Ukat along the way. The trail traverses forests and *padi* fields as well as *kerangas* where pitcher plants and orchids flourish.

Pa'Lungan has a population of 200 residents. A nice refreshing hot shower at the end of the walk is not possible as the community here survives on cold water only. After resting, trekkers are guided to Sarawak's mini Stonehenge of ancient megaliths known as Batu Ritong. Guests can dine here on freshly hunted wild boar and Bario's famous upland rice.

It is also possible to trek from Bario to the summit of Mount Murud (2,423m, 7,950ft), Sarawak's highest peak. However, this is a five-day walk through the steep hills of the Tama Abo Range of Pulong Tau National Park. Other walks include one that heads eastward from Bario into the Apo Kayan Plateau of the Kayan Mentarang National Park in neighbouring North Kalimantan.

This is a sparsely settled transnational area shared between Malaysia and Indonesia in what is known as the 'Heart of Borneo' (see p. 18).

The walk between Ba'Kelalan and Bario passes through Indonesian territory and the village of Long Bawan in Kalimantan is close to Ba'Kelalan. It is important to check on visa requirements before venturing between the two countries.

Getting There

MASwings flies Twin Otter aircraft from Miri and Lawas to Ba'Kelalan and Bario, as well as to smaller communities such as Long Akah, Long Banga, Long Lellang, Long Seridan and Marudi. They may stop at more than one of these destinations on each flight.

The small aircraft definitely offer the quickest way for locals and tourists to get in and out of their remote communities. The alternatives are long, dusty road journeys (12 hours from Miri) and/or boating and

Key Birds of the Kelabit Highlands
Phillipps' Field Guide to the Birds of Borneo notes the following list of montane and submontane birds to be sighted around Bario and the highlands.
Bornean Forktail
Bornean Oriole
Bulwer's Pheasant
Dulit Frogmouth
Hose's Broadbill
Short-tailed Green Magpie
Whitehead's Broadbill
Whitehead's Spiderhunter
Whitehead's Trogon

walking (14 days from Marudi). The arrival of a plane is a time of excitement for the villagers as it provides the main means of connecting them to the outside world. Before a plane arrives a siren is usually sounded, warning everyone to leave the airfield so the plane can land safely.

Where to Stay

Apple Lodge (www.borneoecotours.com)
Pa'Lungun Homestay (www.heartofborneotours.com)

Lun Bawang women in traditional clothes.

BRUNEI DARUSSALAM

Brunei Darussalam is the smallest nation on the island of Borneo. While it is a country that has progressed through its rich oil assets, it has protected much of its natural estate and its pristine forests are some of the best preserved in the region.

Most of Brunei's primary forests remain intact.

Introduction to Brunei Darussalam

At 5,765km^2 (2,226 sq miles), Brunei is Borneo's smallest territory, covering less than 1 per cent of the island's total land surface. It is separated into two distinct parts between the Malaysian state of Sarawak and the towns of Limbang and Lawas (see pp. 116–117). Its maritime border fronts the South China Sea and Brunei Bay, which it shares with the Malaysian Federal Territory of Labuan and the state of Sabah.

Although Brunei is small in size and has a population of just 423,000 inhabitants, the World Bank notes that it has the world's fourth highest per capita GDP due to its extensive petroleum and natural gas reserves, which were discovered in 1929. The main beneficiary is the Sultan of Brunei, Sultan Hassanal Bolkiah, who is considered one of the world's richest men – as witnessed by his lavish official residence, the Istana Nurul Imaan. He is the twenty-ninth sultan and has ruled Brunei since 1967. Brunei's government structure is referred to as a Malay Monarchy, and is ruled according to established Islamic values and traditions.

Previously a powerful regional sultanate, Brunei became a British protectorate in 1888 and remained one until 1984, when it became a self-governing state. Its capital is Bandar Seri Begawan, where 150,000 residents live. Very few Bruneians live in the mountainous and forested eastern region. The other major towns are Muara (a port with ferry connections to Labuan), Seria, Kuala Belait and Panaga. There is an international airport at Berakas, 10 minutes from Bandar Seri Begawan, with Royal Brunei Airlines being the national carrier. Land border crossings into Sabah and Sarawak exist, and Miri is a popular

Small boats provide an important link to Brunei's communities living in water villages.

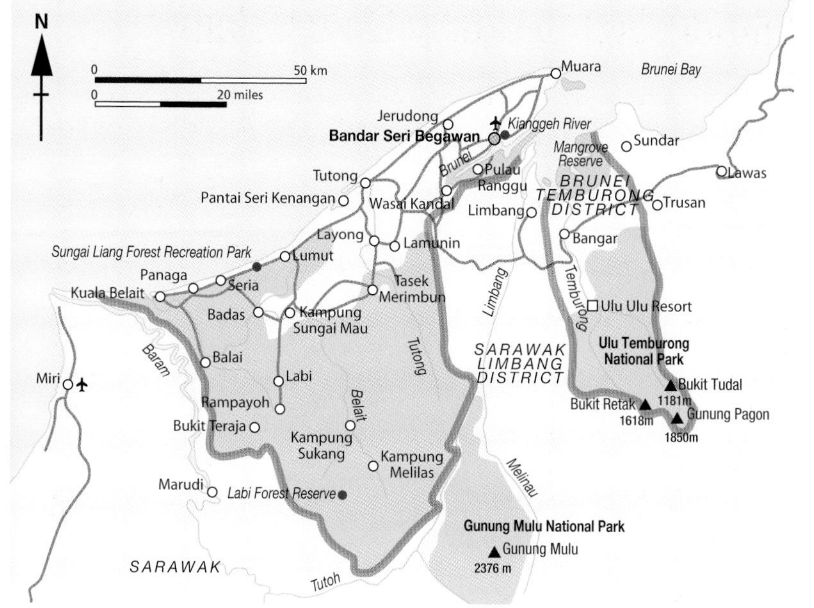

weekend destination. While cowrie shells and bronze teapots were once used for barter trading, the Brunei dollar became the official currency in 1967 and it continues to be linked to the Singapore dollar. Interestingly, Brunei's rarely seen $10,000 note is the world's most valuable banknote. It and the other banknotes of Brunei are now made from polymer.

Bandar Seri Begawan

The capital, located along the Brunei River upstream from Brunei Bay, has a few tourist attractions, ranging from the water village (Kampong Ayer) to religious sites, museums and many pristine forests.

Bandar Seri Begawan is the smallest of all the ASEAN capitals, and many travellers note that it offers a town-like atmosphere rather than that of a capital city.

Sultan Omar Ali Saifuddien Mosque sits like a ship on water and is spectacularly lit up at night as a shining reminder of Islam. It is hard not to be impressed by the scale of what is considered the region's largest mosque. Its gold-covered dome reaches a height of 52m (171ft), and it is supported by columns, arches and towers with marble walls. Stained-glass windows from England and carpets from Saudi Arabia are other decorative features. Built in 1958, the mosque is situated on an artificial lagoon near the Brunei River in the capital, and is named after Brunei's twenty-eighth sultan.

A popular place for visitors is Kampong Ayer, or Water Village, perched over water along the banks of the Brunei River. It is home to 30,000 permanent residents and is accessible via wooden bridges and boats. Wooden boardwalks weave through the riverside maze, and visitors are free to roam and explore. In addition to the houses, there are schools, clinics, shops and mosques.

Other attractions in the capital include the Royal Regalia Musem, the Brunei History Centre, Tasek Recreational Park and Brunei Museum. Tamu Kianggeh is a local market located in the centre of the capital on the banks of the Kianggeh River. Open daily from early until late, it is the venue for fresh produce.

Coastal Areas

There is a 160-km (100-mile) stretch of beach in the larger western section of Brunei. Pantai Tutong, Pantai Seri Kenangan and Kuala Tutong are casuarina-lined beachfronts backed by the Tutong River.

The sprawling seaside Empire Hotel and Country Club fronting the South China Sea at Jerudong features extravagant suites and rooms, but guests also have the option of swimming in eight hotel pools. It is a mini-entertainment city with a ten-pin bowling alley, cinema, championship golf course and restaurants. Along the hotel's beachfront there is a multitude of watersports from jet skiing, parasailing and sailing, to diving in the waters off the beach. This grand property is not only Brunei's largest hotel; it is a destination in itself some 30 minutes' drive from the capital.

The Sultan Omar Ali Saifuddin Mosque set in its own lake.

Jerudong Park Playground is an ambitious fun theme park that opened with a big splash in 1994. Now somewhat scaled back, the park opens mostly at the weekends and offers rides, a water park, mini-golf, Ferris wheel, pedal boats, an amphitheatre for concerts and a food court. Phase Two includes a Scary Drop ride, two new water rides, an area with a zipline and a pirate ship.

Sungai Liang Forest Recreation Park is a popular coastal recreational forest area covered in lowland forest that has nature trails, a canopy walkway and interpretation material. It also provides access to the Andulau Forest Reserve.

Emergent trees in Brunei's rainforest.

Brunei, Naturally

While it is best known for its vast oil reserves, Brunei also has some of the region's best-preserved tropical forests. An estimated 80 per cent of Brunei has forest cover, with 60 per cent of it still intact. This has become increasingly important to scientists as other forests around the region are modified.

Brunei is home to the last and vast intact rainforest on Borneo's west coast. Ecologically important tracts of beaches lined with casuarinas, peat-swamp forest, lowland dipterocarp forest, heath forest and freshwater-swamp forest also thrive in Brunei. Belait peat-swamp forest in the far west of Brunei is one of the best

Entrance to Jerudong Park Playground.

examples of this threatened forest type along Borneo's west coast. River safaris journeying several hours up the Belait River to Dusun and Penan communities living at Kampong Sukang are available.

Labi Forest Reserve, drained by the Belait River and contiguous with Gunung Mulu National Park in neighbouring Sarawak (see pp. 38–39) features virgin mixed dipterocarp forest, patches of freshwater-swamp forest and upland heath forest. Millions of insectivorous bats, including those from neighbouring Mulu, feed in these Bruneian forests.

With these two parks separated by only the Melinau River, there is the possibility of a large transboundary protected area being established. Interestingly, no Orangutans are found in Brunei's forests and it is thought that they were hunted to extinction. Scientists believe various other threatened mammals could be reintroduced into a large transboundary park if created.

Temburong

Brunei's eastern part is known as Temburong District, and much of it is still under green cover. Bangar is the main town in the east, and is accessible by boat from the capital. Even on this journey there is the opportunity to spot wildlife, including crocodiles sunning themselves along the riverbanks.

Much of this part of Brunei is undeveloped, and its forests are home to Iban, Murut and Malay people. It is also home to Brunei's first national park, Ulu Temburong, covering 50,000ha (123,553 acres) of primary rainforest, just one hour's boat ride from the capital. Its proximity to civilization makes it one of the region's most accessible wilderness areas.

Located within Batu Apoi Forest Reserve, plant communities in the park range from lowland dipterocarp forest through to montane forests at an altitude of 1,800m (5,900ft). There are no roads in the park and access is via longboat along the Temburong River or by forest trails. The Belalong area is devoted entirely to scientific research, and the Kuala Belalong Field Studies Centre is home to local and international academics and scientists. Visitors can stay in Ulu Ulu Resort located on the opposite riverbank.

The resort has adopted various green and socially responsible practices. Accommodation is provided in dormitories plus twin and double rooms and there is a cafe serving locally sourced produce, a gift shop, meeting room, indoor cinema and a meeting hall. Activities include trekking, a visit to a waterfall, a canopy walk and a night jungle walk.

Boardwalks lead into the rainforest and to the Belalong Canopy Walk for a unique 50m (160ft) high aerial view of the misty forests. While not an easy walk in the heat and humidity, it is worth the effort. Treehouses connected via hanging bridges are useful for wildlife spotting and photography. Observant visitors may get a glimpse of the rare and endemic Hose's Langur, or butterflies such as the large and colourful Rajah Brooke's Birdwing.

Accommodation (guest houses and campsites) is also available at the park headquarters. Some trekking companies have their own accommodation, boats and guides, and can offer short or extended treks through the park; independent travellers should use a nature guide. Access to the park is via ferryboats that travel along mangrove-lined waterways and creeks.

Mangroves are an important habitat in this part of Brunei.Some 18,500ha (21,000 acres) line Brunei River and its mouth at Muara. This is the largest protected mangrove habitat on Borneo's west coast. Brunei Bay also contains the largest seagrass beds along the west of Borneo providing feeding grounds for Dugongs.

Islands in the bay are important resting sites for migratory birds travelling southwards for the warmer climate of the European winter, especially from September to April. These birds start their long journeys in places like Japan, Russia and China. Raptors such as the Brahminy Kite and White-bellied Sea-eagle are often seen soaring overhead, catching fish or resting among the mangroves.

Getting There

Access to the park is via a series of boats from the capital to Bangar, then Ulu Temburong, and then via long boat. The whole journey takes almost two hours.

Where to Stay

Ulu Ulu National Park Resort
(www.uluuluresort.com)
Forestry Department
(www.forestry.gov.bn)
Empire Hotel and Country Club
(www.theempire.com)

The misty rainforests of Ulu Temburong.

KALIMANTAN

Kalimantan is the name given to the Indonesian part of the island of Borneo. It occupies 73 per cent of the island's total land area, mostly in the southern part of Borneo. The word 'Kalimantan' is derived from Sanskrit for 'burning weather island'. Administratively, there are five provinces – North, East, South, West and Central.

Derawan Island in the Celebes Sea.

Introduction to Kalimantan

Kalimantan is home to numerous indigenous groups and its abundant natural resources have attracted many outsiders throughout its history, including the Chinese, Dutch and Japanese (see pp. 14-15).

Another important historical event in Kalimantan was the Indonesia-Malaysia Confrontation (Konfrontasi), which was a violent conflict that raged between 1963 and 1966. Indonesia opposed the creation of Malaysia, especially the inclusion of British Borneo (North Borneo, or modern-day Sabah and Sarawak) in the federation. Most of the warfare extended along the British Borneo/Kalimantan border, but ceased when Indonesia recognized the Malaysian Federation in 1966.

The majority of the 15 million people living in Kalimantan embrace Islam, Buddhism or Christianity, and the official language is Bahasa Indonesia. While some people still live a traditional lifestyle in remote areas, the bulk of the Indonesians in Kalimantan live in cities like Tarakan, Balikpapan, Banjarmasin, Palangkaraya and Pontianak.

The Natural World

Most visitors travel to Kalimantan because it is remote, isolated and has wondrous flora and fauna within rainforests dating back 130 million years. While parts of Kalimantan (covering 544,150km²/210,097 sq miles) remain undeveloped, there is growing environmental concern about logging (legal and illegal), and the expansion of oil-palm and pulpwood forests in Kalimantan.

In nature, decaying vegetation beneath peat forests breaks down and becomes part of the soil, but when it is drained and dried it becomes vulnerable to fire. The peat in the soil can burn for a long time and is difficult to extinguish, with the resultant

At night, Pontianak is a colourful river port city.

smoke creating disastrous and dangerous conditions. Forest fires arising from the burning of peat-swamp forests have become all too common in recent years, causing the region to be blanketed in a smoky haze.

Efforts have been made to preserve several important ecological areas in Kalimantan, and various transborder national parks are planned with neighbouring Malaysia.

Some leading national parks and reserves include Ketapang Orangutan Rehabilitation Centre (see pp. 34–35), Lamandau River Wildlife Reserve (see pp. 144–145), Tanjung Puting National Park (see pp. 34–35 and 144–145), Kutai National Park (see pp. 136–137) and Kayan Mentarang National Park (see pp. 136–137). Several of these protected natural areas are located in isolated parts of Kalimantan, and transportation to these parks and accommodation in them offer few comforts or luxuries. However, this is what makes them so appealing to intrepid travellers.

North Kalimantan

Indonesia's newest province of North Kalimantan was created in 2012; before that it was part of East Kalimantan. It has a long mountainous border with the Malaysian states of Sabah and Sarawak, but with no recognized land border crossings. Covering 72, 275km² (27,906 sq miles), the state has few major settlements. Some 630,000 people live in North Kalimantan, with a third of residents living in Tarakan., a town situated on an island of the same name at the mouth of the Kayan River, which splits into several channels at its swampy delta on the southwestern coastline. Tarakan is home to the Tidung people, who originated in the north-east of Borneo, and even across the Celebes and Sulu Seas into the southern Philippines.

After the discovery of oil, Tarakan became strategically important during the Dutch East Indies' colonial days, and it was one of the first targets for invading Japanese forces during the Second World War. Australian forces recaptured Tarakan in 1945, and there is a memorial in the city recognizing their efforts.

There are a few attractions around Tarakan, including Tarakan Mangrove Conservation Park, which has elevated boardwalk trails across the swampy land. Amal Beach on the east coast is the most popular beach on the island. Elevated views of the city, island and coastline are possible from Mount Putih on the mainland to the south-west of Tarakan.

Forested Hinterland

North Kalimantan's isolated interior has ensured that some of Borneo's most pristine forests are protected in the province's mountainous parts. Kayan Mentarang National Park of 1.36 million hectares (3.36 million acres) stretches along much of the border with Sarawak and

Waterfall in Mentarang National Park.

There are pleasant beaches near Tarakan where it's good to take a swim.

Sabah and has a wealth of flora and fauna, including at least 150 mammals and 300 species of bird. This really is the heart of Borneo and the headwaters for several of Borneo's mighty rivers. Mount Harun at 2,160m (7,087ft), near the Sarawak/Sabah border, is the highest peak.

The Sarawakian outposts of Ba'Kelalan and Bario are located on the Malaysian side of the border but close to the park's western boundary. The park is home to a small number of Lun Bawang, Penan and Kenyah people, some of whom have an affinity with their Malaysian neighbours.

These communities still practise subsistence hunting, but there are some concerns about illegally poached forest products. This trade is not new and has been part of forest life for the past 1,000 years, with products such as rhinoceros horns, hornbill casques and swiftlet nests among many other items following a well-defined trading route to southern China.

Getting There

Visitors arriving from Tawau in the far east of Sabah travel into North Kalimantan and the provincial capital of Tarakan via ferry. Nunukan Island across from Tawau is also a ferry hub to several other Indonesian destinations. MASwings flies between Tawau and Tarakan.

Where to Stay

Visits to the park and the homestay accommodation in it are best arranged in Samarinda, although a few forest trails also extend across the border into Bario and Ba'Kelalan – an Indonesian visa needs to be obtained before any such trek.

East Kalimantan

The province of East Kalimantan covers an area of 129,067km^2 (49,833 sq miles), and its capital Samarinda is home to 850,000 residents. Its easternmost parts front the Makassar Strait and the Celebes Sea (or Sulawesi Sea), while its remote northwestern boundary borders Sarawak.

East Kalimantan is a resource-rich province, with coal and gold mines plus valuable oil reserves. Coastal Balikpapan with 650,000 residents has an oil refinery and coal is exported from the port. River transport into the hinterland is a necessity for many of the locals, as well as being an attraction for visitors. Samarinda is the starting point for journeys on the Mahakam River and associated lakes.

Waterbirds are abundant on the lakes, especially during the dry season in July and August. Irrawaddy Dolphins and crocodiles also live in the lake.

Protected Areas

Sungai Wain is home to the single most important stand of lowland dipterocarp forest in the province. Despite having been affected by past fires, it is ecologically significant for its high diversity of plants, mammals and birds; being one hour from Balikpapan, it is one of Borneo's most accessible forests. While homestays near the park are possible, most visitors come here on a day visit from Balikpapan. Birdwatchers can relish the opportunity to sight the Borneo Peacock Pheasant in what is considered the only accessible location in Borneo.

Samboja Lestari Wildlife Reserve, one hour from Balikpapan, has an Orangutan and Sun Bear rescue and rehabilitation centre. Samboja Lodge offers good accommodation and half-day tours (morning or afternoon). A longer visit that includes wildlife spotting from a boat along the river is possible. The

Islands in the Derawan Group are some of the most picturesque on Borneo's east coast.

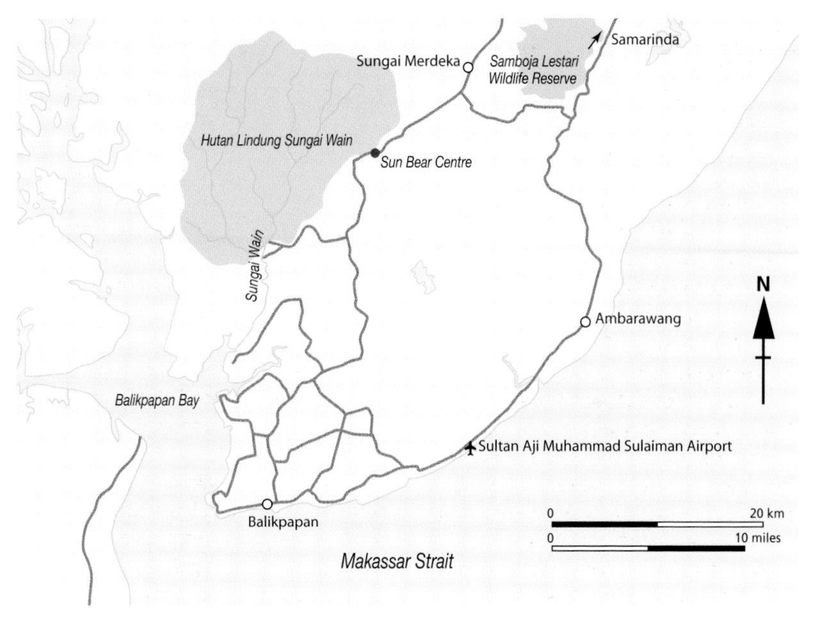

Samboja Lestari Wildlife Reserve.

lodge can arrange ecotours in the district, including a visit to Sungai Wain and a treetop canopy walk in Bukit Bengkirai.

Kutai National Park is located north of Samarinda and Bontang, just north of the Equator. While parts of it have been logged and mined, there are reasonable stands of lowland forests and several lakes (*danau* in Bahasa). WWF have captured footage of possibly two wild Sumatran Rhinoceroses in the park and suggest that they are the last wild rhinos in Borneo.

Mangroves and Islands

Balikpapan Bay supports mangroves that are home to some 1,400 Proboscis Monkeys, one of Borneo's biggest populations.

While the beaches along coastal parts are pleasant enough, sun seekers should head to islands in the Celebes Sea, such as Kakaban Island in the Derawan Group. There are 31 islands (ranging in size from 2ha/5 acres, to Maratua Island, which is the largest at 2,376ha/5,871 acres). They are located just offshore where East Kalimantan becomes North Kalimantan. The main approach is from Tarakan.

Getting There

Balikpapan's Sultan Aji Muhammad Sulaiman Airport (formerly Sepinggan Airport) is the international air gateway to East Kalimantan, and a major airport for *haj* pilgrims flying to Mecca. There are direct flights from Singapore (on SilkAir), Jakarta and other Indonesian destinations.

Where to Stay

Samboja Lodge
(www.sambojalodge.com)

South Kalimantan

This province occupies the far south-east of the island of Borneo and supports a population of 3.9 million people, of which 675,000 live in the provincial capital of Banjarmasin on the eastern bank of the Barito River. South Kalimantan comprises an area of 38,744km^2 (14,959 sq miles), with almost half the province being flat and covered in alluvial land or swamp. While South Kalimantan is the smallest province, its capital is the largest city in Kalimantan and is served by Syamsudin Noor Airport.

Like many rivers in the province, the Barito River rises in the Meratus Mountains and drains into the Java Sea to the south. Other rivers drain eastwards into the Makassar Strait, which separates the province from Indonesian Sulawesi.

Meratus Mountains

The Meratus Mountains, aligned north-south in South Kalimantan's eastern parts, are more hilly than mountainous, rising up to Mount Besar at 1,892m (6,207ft). Stands of hill and montane forest cover the mountains – they are mostly unprotected.

Jungle trekking to Dayak communities and mountain climbing attract adventurers, while rafting and tubing down rivers is also possible. Loksado, some three and a half hours' drive from Banjarmasin, is the place to head to for an adventurous holiday staying in simple accommodation offered at Meratus Resort, in Dayak longhouse accommodation or in homestays. Engaging the services of a trekking company or local guide is important, as many trails criss-cross the mountains.

Just as in many rainforests, it is not always the large animals that will be spotted, but rather the smaller species such as insects, fungi and flowers. Among the moths, look out for the large Atlas Moth.

The Martapura River at the south-western extent of the Meratus Mountains was dammed in order to generate hydropower. The 8,000ha (19,764-acre) Lake Riam Kanan is now a popular tourist attraction, with Bukit Matang Kaladan being the departure point for boat journeys across the lake. Bukit Batas (Batas Hill) is a population venue for camping and watching the sun rise.

To Market

Lok Baintan Floating Market selling fresh fruits and vegetables takes place near Banjarmasin on the Martapura River, and is a big attraction accessible by local *klotok* boats. It is best to go in the early morning darkness as it takes one hour to travel there by boat from the city, and the market is mostly finished by 8.30 a.m. – after that it also gets too hot. While there are some tourist boats, this is very much a market for the locals who live along the canals connected to the river.

Martapura River is a main transportation route upstream and into Central Kalimantan, as are other rivers.

Where to Stay

Mercure Banjarmasin
(www.mercure.accorhotels.com)
Mount Meratus Resort
(www.mountmeratusresort.com)

The floating market near Banjarmasin is unique in Borneo.

West Kalimantan

West Kalimantan (Kalimantan Barat) is located in the south-west of Borneo. Its western coastline fronts the South China Sea, and its southern parts the Java Sea. The Karimata Strait separates West Kalimantan from several neighbouring Indonesian islands, including Sumatra. The province is dissected by the Equator, with the capital city Pontianak sitting right on the Equator.

Covering an area of 147,308km^2 (56,876 sq miles), much of the interior is forested and remote. River access along the Kapuas River is important for those living in the interior. At 1,143km (710 miles) in length and originating in the Müller mountain range, the Kapuas River is the longest in Indonesia, although confusingly there is a river of the same name that originates on the other side of the range and flows southwards before emptying into the Java Sea.

The province's ecology includes wetlands, rivers and lakes, plus peat-swamp and mangrove forests, but forest clearing has taken its toll on the primary forests. WWF has noted that 56 per cent of the protected lowland tropical rainforests in the whole of Kalimantan were cut down between 1985 and 2001 to satisfy the global demand for timber. While laws to protect these forests were in place, they proved inadequate in saving this valuable resource.

Now the global demand for palm oil has resulted in the expansion of oil-palm plantations throughout Kalimantan and the rest of Borneo.

West Kalimantan has a population of 4.55 million residents who have Dayak, Malay, Javanese and Chinese heritage. Chinese miners were the first migrants to settle among the local Dayaks, and they even established what was known as the Lanfang Republic. This was replaced by Dutch rule

The Raya Mujahidin Mosque in Pontianak.

in 1884, and in the 1930s the colonialists encouraged transmigration from the more crowded islands like Java. In the 1960s, transmigration of people from the island of Madura also occurred, but not without hostilities between them and the locals.

Pontianak, the Capital

In Bahasa, *pontianak* refers to a mythical female vampire ghost, and the city's name is attributed to such a spirit that supposedly haunted the first sultan.

West Kalimantan has many rivers – the Kapuas River divides into several branches on its delta, and Pontianak is spread along three of these branches. Taman Alun-alun Kapuas is a popular park on the river's southern bank. There is bustling river activity, with goods and people constantly passing through on journeys via the sea.

The Equator Monument stands just outside the city centre, and while it is not exactly on the Equator (the monument has moved slightly from where it was originally built), it is near enough. There are two museums in the city – the Museum of West Kalimantan and the Orangutan Museum. The former provides good information on the people of the province, mainly the Dayaks, Malays and Chinese.

Major religious places include St Joseph's Cathedral and Masjid Raya Mujahidin. The current cathedral dates back to as recently as 2014, and replaced the smaller and original structure built in 1908. The mosque is the city's largest and most ornately decorated, with a copper-covered dome, four gold-topped minarets and a large tower in the front. Tthe open space surrounding the mosque is a popular meeting and recreational area for the locals. Istana Kadriah is a small palace that was home to the former rulers of Pontianak.

The Equator Monument.

ParadiseQ Waterpark is open daily from morning until early evening. It has slides, glides, rides and pools for cooling off in the tropical heat.

The Interior

Danau (Lake) Sentarum National Park, situated in the heart of Borneo and covering 1,320km^2 (510 sq miles), protects one of the world's most diverse lake ecosystems. It is a Ramsar Site with a recorded 237 bird species, including the endangered and rarely seen Storm's Stork (the species is thought to breed in Tanjung Puting). It is also home to the Proboscis Monkey and Estuarine Crocodile.

Ferries provide access to different parts of Pontianak.

This volcanic depression becomes a vast floodplain during the wet season, even though the lake is located 700km (435 miles) upstream along the Kapuas River. More than 200 fish species have been recorded here, and the park is home to traditional fishing people.

Betung Kerihun National Park, covering an area of 8,000km^2 (3,100 sq miles) north-east of Putussibau, is a mountainous park proposed as a transborder park with Lanjak Entimau Wildlife Sanctuary and Batang Ai National Park in neighbouring Sarawak. This Indonesian park is just 60km (37 miles) south of Sarawak's Kapit, located along the Rajang River. The park is the source of the Kapuas River and is home to montane forest in the higher altitudes.

Coastal Areas

Pantai Pesisir, located near Singkawang, 140km (87 miles) north of Pontianak, is a popular beach with watersports and cafes..

Gunung Palung National Park of 900km^2 (350 sq miles) is located on and around Mount (Gunung) Palung and Mount Panti near the coast between Pontianak and Ketapang. The area was first protected in 1937 as a forest reserve (the area was then a third of what it is today), increased in size and revised to a wildlife reserve in 1981 before being gazetted a national park in 1990. The park is one of the least accessible in Kalimantan and is best suited to adventurous travellers who have a little extra time on their hands.

The park supports a diversity of natural habitats that rivals virtually anywhere else on the island of Borneo. Mount Palung (1,100m, 3,609 ft) rises up from flat, swampy lowlands through to dry dipterocarp forest and then montane forest near the summit. The lowland areas include beaches and forests dominated by mangroves, peat and freshwater swamp species. The park is home to key species such as the Orangutan, Bornean Sun Bear, White-handed Gibbon, Proboscis Monkey, Horsfield's Tarsier and Sunda Pangolin. Scientists suggest that the park contains ten per cent of the world's wild Orangutan population. Most of Borneo's lowland bird species are found here; the list includes rarities such as Bornean Peacock Pheasants, Bornean Bristleheads and White-headed Hornbills.

Environmentalists are concerned that the park's buffer zone has been illegally logged with some 40 per cent of the core area also having been logged.

Cabang Panti Research Centre was established in the park to provide valuable information on the rainforest ecology. There are trails radiating from the centre through all of the forest habitatss.

Visitors need to register at park offices at Melano, Ketapang or Sukadana and rangers can assist with identifying guides to lead a visit into the park.

Getting There

There are several border crossings into neighbouring Sarawak, and roads connect the province to the southern parts of Central Kalimantan. Supadio International Airport on the outskirts of Pontianak services flights from several airports in Indonesia, including Jakarta, as well as international flights from Singapore and Kuching.

For Danau Sentarum National Park, most visitors travel by road or fly to Putussibau (east), or by road to Sintang (south-west); from both it is another seven-hour boat journey into the park.

For Gunung Palung National Park, most journeys start in Pontianak and on to Ketapang and then Sukadana before a long boat ride into the park.

Where to Stay

Tanjung Bajau Resort
(www.tanjungbajauresort.com)

The fastest way to connect to areas in riverine Pontianak is by small boats powered by outboard motors.

Central Kalimantan

Central Kalimantan encompasses 153,566km[2] (59,292 sq miles). Much of it was once covered in primary forest, but a great deal of the province has been cleared and is covered with secondary forest.

Palangkaraya with 260,000 residents lies in an upstream region of the Kahayan River. It is the provincial capital and where the Balanga Museum offers a window on the local Dayak community. Traditional dances such as the Giring-Giring are performed here to a rhythmic bell sound.

Pangkalan Bun (Pangkalanbun) has a population of 200,000 and is home to two sultan's palaces, including the Yellow Palace. Churches and mosques stand side by side, and a boat journey along the river offers an insight on those who live here.

Many visitors arrive here and head off to discover Tanjung Puting National Park and the popular Camp Leakey, which was established by the Canadian-born anthropologist and President of Orangutan Foundation International, Dr Biruté Galdikas, in the 1970s. The park is considered to be Kalimantan's most important wildlife tourism site. Located 100km (60 miles) by road and boat from Pangkalan Bun, Camp Leakey and its rehabilitation site offer excellent facilities for observing Orangutans in the wild. The park also supports a variety of forest types, including peat-swamp forest, *kerangas* (heath), wetlands and lowland forest, which are home to populations of Red Langur,

Orangutans ensure Tanjung Puting is Kalimantan's most important wildlife tourism site.

White-bearded Gibbon and Proboscis Monkey. For birdwatchers, many species of hornbill and kingfisher are the main attractions. There are also large numbers of breeding herons, and the rare Storm's Stork, Bornean Bristlehead and Lesser Adjutant have been recorded in the park.

Access to the Lamandau Wildlife Reserve (see pp. 36–37) is via Pangkalan Bun or Kumai. The reserve is a location for native and rehabilitated Orangutans.

Sabangau is another large national park in the province, located to the east of both Lamandau and Tanjung Puting. It supports extensive stands of peat-swamp forest, and boardwalks provide access to some parts that are often flooded. Unfortunately, large tracts of the forest were destroyed to facilitate the failed Mega Rice Project.

Swampy land here works to the advantage of wildlife, since it is difficult for humans to penetrate and to farm. As a result, scientists have noticed high concentrations of mammals such as Orangutans. The peat-swamp forests also fruit throughout the year, providing food for up to an estimated 7,000 Orangutans. One of the best ways to admire the wildlife is to take a boat cruise. The Katingan River of 600km (373 miles) in length forms part of the park's western border.

Exploring Tanjung Puting is done at a leisurely pace in a boat.

Getting There

Travellers can fly into Pangkalan Bun or travel on ferries that cross the Karimata Strait to Java.

Where to Stay

Rimba Ecolodge
(www.rimbaecolodge.com)

PART 3: TRAVEL MATTERS

Small planes ensure remote communities remain in touch with the outside world.

Practicalities

Many people travel to Borneo because it is considered to be one of the last frontiers of tourism. It is mostly off the main tourist trails, is less frequently visited than other places, and often involves long and adventurous journeys into places where few venture. Knowing the basics is important in order to save valuable time and maximize experiences on this wondrous island. While there are many similarities between the parts of Borneo, there are also numerous differences that travellers need to be aware of as they travel through Malaysia, Brunei and Indonesian Kalimantan.

Entry Requirements

Visas may be required for some nationalities; check with the respective countries before departure. Passports require six months' validity and at least two blank pages. They need to be carried at all times as proof of identity, and spare passport photos are always useful. Border crossings between Sarawak and Kalimantan can be problematic, and the remotest ones cannot issues visas, so check first and obtain a visa from either an Indonesian or a Malaysian embassy (depending on the travel route) before travelling.

- **Brunei** 14-, 30- and 90-day visas are issued to some 50 nationalities. For example, visa-free entry is available to citizens of Britain, the USA and the EU (90 days), Malaysia, Singapore and New Zealand (30 days), and ASEAN, Canada and Japan (14 days). For a fee, visas are issued on arrival to Australians, Chinese and Taiwanese.
- **Malaysia** Both Sarawak and Sabah operate their own customs and immigration independently, but in conjunction with the system in West Malaysia. Most tourists to Sarawak and Sabah receive 90-day visas.
- **Indonesian Kalimantan** 30-day tourist visas are issued to most nationalities on arrival.

Health

Borneo straddles the Equator and numerous tropical diseases are prevalent, although the situation is perhaps not as bad as many people may think. Precautions against malaria and dengue fever should be taken, and medical advice sought as both are complex diseases.

Both are spread by mosquitoes so avoiding them is the best solution. However, in the tropics, this is easier said than done as cases of dengue fever have risen drastically around the globe in the past decades. Spread by the Aedes mosquito some 100,000 cases are reported each year in Malaysia alone with 329 per 100,000 people affected. Known as 'break-bone fever' its symptoms include high fever, headaches, muscle and joint pain, several days of lethargy, and hot and cold flushes. Fortunately, it is not contagious from person to person. Visitors to Borneo should not be alarmed if they occasionally see what looks to be clouds of smoke emerging from buildings at either dusk or dawn. Known as fogging, machines cast a mist of insecticide that knocks down adult mosquitoes and assists in the reduction of their numbers.

Prevention is the best remedy. Mosquitoes are most active at dawn and dusk, so it is best, especially for those prone to mosquito attack, to stay indoors during these times. Most longhouses that welcome visitors will be equipped with mosquito nets for sleeping beneath.

Wearing loose clothing to cover parts of the body like ankles is advisable as is using an insect spray. Burning mosquito coils is another way of keeping these insects at bay.

Travelling with a small personal first aid kit with basic medical equipment is also advisable especially for those visiting remote areas – plasters, gauze, cotton wool, thermometer, rolled bandages, swabs, tweezers, sterile rubber gloves, scissors, sterile swabs, antiseptic cream and basic painkillers.

With many parts of Borneo covered in vegetation, it should come as no surprise that animals living here include venomous snakes. Few visitors will actually encounter one as they tend to stay out of the way, but caution should be exercised all the same. Most snakes are well camouflaged, making them difficult to see. Covering the arms and legs with light clothing is recommended.

Many remote locations have rudimentary medical facilities such as a nurse, clinic and visiting doctors. Flights to the outside world may at best be every few days, so remote Borneo is not a place in which to get sick or have a misadventure. Travel insurance is always recommended – reading the fine print is advisable for those participating in adventurous activities.

Money

Cash is always king but there are ATMs, moneychangers and banks as a back-up. The official currency is the Brunei dollar (pegged to the Singapore dollar) in Brunei, the ringgit in Malaysia and the rupiah in Indonesia. The banking hours are:

- **Malaysia** Monday to Friday, 9.15 a.m. to 4.30 p.m.
- **Brunei** Monday to Friday, 9 a.m. to 3 p.m., Saturday 8 a.m. to noon.
- **Indonesia** Monday to Friday, 8 a.m. to 3 p.m. and Saturday, 8 a.m. to 1 p.m.

Credit cards

Credit cards are accepted in many establishments in all large towns and cities in Borneo. Using them could be challenging in smaller villages and almost impossible in remote longhouses. Cash is necessary in these small places with the currency of each particular nation the best (for example, in Malaysia the ringgit is basically the only currency accepted by businesses and traders and foreign currency would need to be changed at a bank or a money changer). Some smaller business may add a surcharge (up to 3 per cent) for using a credit card.

Tipping is not a common practice in Borneo and a service tax and relevant government taxes are imposed anyway in most parts of the island in substantive outlets (rarely markets). Visitors who receive exceptional service especially from tour guides, who escort them for several days, may consider rewarding these people and these tips will be graciously accepted.

Some tour operators and guides take small gifts to remote longhouses as a token of thanks for them receiving visitors. However, in some cases, they may buy junk food such as biscuits, snack foods and soft drinks. Visitors who find this unacceptable should insist upon something more wholesome or beneficial to the community. Stationery items such as pencils, rulers, books and erasers make suitable gifts that will be well received and useful to the children of these villages.

Business and Shopping Hours

Most businesses are open on Monday to Friday from 9 a.m. to 5 p.m., and possibly for half a day on Saturday. Some may close from noon to 3 p.m. on Friday for prayers. Shopping centres in big cities are normally open daily from 10 a.m. to 10 p.m.

Climate

As a general rule the climate is hot and humid year round. High-altitude locations such as Mount Kinabalu can be quite cold, and those attempting the summit climb need to come prepared for overnight temperatures of zero degrees. Monsoonal winds affect different parts of Borneo at different times of the year. While there are regional differences, monsoon rains fall between November and April, with the dry season being from May to October.

Most storms are short and days of lingering rain are rare. The locals are used to this and simply seek shelter when it rains as they know the storm will pass over. Meanwhile, motorcyclists put on their wet weather gear or take cover. Visitors should do the same but taking a raincoat or fold-up umbrella is also advisable. Flash flooding is another problem travellers need to be aware of and they should avoid crossing swollen streams until they subside.

Public Holidays

It is worth noting that some holiday dates change from year to year.

All of Borneo	
New Year's Day	1 January
Chinese New Year	January/February
Good Friday	March/April
Gawai/Harvest Festival	May/June
Hari Raya Puasa	June
Hari Raya Aidiladha	August/September
Muslim New Year	September/October
Prophet's Birthday	December
Christmas Day	25 December
Sarawak and Sabah	
Wesak Day (Buddha's Birthday)	May
King's Birthday	June
Independence Day	31 August
Malaysia Day	23 October
Brunei	
Brunei National Day	23 February
Sultan of Brunei's Birthday	15 July
Kalimantan	
Waisak (Buddha's Birthday)	May
Independence Day	17 August

Tourist Offices Overseas

Malaysia

Tourism Malaysia has several offices overseas with a full list available at: www.malaysia.travel.
Its key offices are:
Auckland (New Zealand) - +649 309-6290
Bangkok (Thailand) - +662 636-3380
Hong Kong (China) +852 2528-5810
Johannesburg (South Africa) – +2711 268-6290
London (UK) - +44 207 9307
Los Angeles (USA) – +1 213 689-9702
New York (USA) – +1 212 754-1113
Sydney (Australia) – +612 9286-3055

Brunei

Brunei Tourism Department (www.bruneitourism.travel)

Indonesia

Indonesia Travel has several offices overseas with a full list available at www.indonesia.travel). Its key offices are:
Amsterdam (The Netherlands) – +31 20 670-5211
Hong Kong (China) - +852 2793-9998
London (UK) - +44 203 375-4050
Melbourne (Australia) - +61 3 9005-6634
Sydney (Australia) - +61 41 942-5455

Consulates

Several countries have consulates or honorary consulates where travellers can seek travel assistance or information on the country. Contact the following:

in Kota Kinabalu
Australia - +60 88 267-151
Brunei - +60 88 236-112
United Kingdom - + 60 88 251-775

in Kuching
Australia - +60 82 230-777
Brunei - +60 82 417-616
Indonesia - +60 82 460-734

in Tawau
Indonesia - +60 89 772-052

Religion and Festivals

While many tribal groups in Borneo were originally animists, most are now nominally followers of the great global religions – Islam, Hinduism, Christianity, Buddhism and Taoism. However, in addition to following religious guidance and direction, many people still believe in spirits, as well as the importance of their ancestors. They put trust in traditional medicine as administered by a *bomoh*, or medicine man.

Ritual observance is an essential part of life for most people in many parts of Borneo, especially in rural and remote districts. It manifests itself in etiquette, law, marriage, relationships, family interrelationships and many other aspects of daily life.

Rituals are usually performed by shamans, priests, village leaders or elders. Sacrifices of animals are still an important element of life for many villagers.

Typically, when someone relocates from one village to another, especially on the occasion of their marriage, they tend to take on the rituals and customs of their adopted village.

Christianity (both Anglicanism and Roman Catholicism) was introduced into North Sabah (then North Borneo) in 1882 via the British North Borneo Chartered Company. In Sarawak, Rajah James Brooke supported an Anglican mission from as early as 1847 and the Dutch allowed missionaries into parts of Kalimantan after 1836.

While just 9 per cent of Malaysians are nominally Christian, two-thirds of their numbers reside in East Malaysia, in Sarawak and Sabah, where they comprise some 30 per cent of the total population. Estimates also suggest that 25 to 35 per cent of the population of West, East and Central Kalimantan are Christians.

Holidays and Festivals

Most festivals in Borneo involve a holiday with a day or more off work. Many of these occasions are ceremonial and celebrate symbolic events in villages.

Gawai Dayak, Pesta Ka'amatan

One of the most important festivals in Sarawak and Kalimantan is Gawai Dayak, which marks the end of the rice harvest and is celebrated in early June. At a similar time, Sabahans celebrate Pesta Ka'amatan, or the Harvest Festival, to show appreciation for a bountiful rice harvest.

Like many other holidays in Borneo, people return to their village and family home to make the most of the break. Family reunions are important and the opportunity is taken to visit parents, siblings and extended family and to relax. This normally means lots of eating, resting, children playing, dressing up in traditional clothes, singing and reminiscing.

In some communities, rice wine or *tuak* brewed from glutinous rice, plays a role. There are many names for this alcoholic spirit in different parts of Borneo (*lihing*, *talak* and *tapai*). Cassava is also used as an ingredient in *tapai*, the preferred party beverage of the Murut in Sabah.

Prior to the mid-year festivities, longhouses are cleaned, larders restocked and wild animals may be hunted for their meat. At the beginning of the festivities, rituals are performed, offerings are made to various spirits and thanks are given for the good harvest. A celebratory and communal meal is enjoyed on the first evening along the verandah of the longhouse. Afterwards, there is singing, poetry reading and dancing.

On the second day, guests are invited to join in the celebrations with 'open house' invitations being extended to those living outside the immediate community. This is the time that travellers will be welcomed but they need to be warned that numerous 'watering' activities may be involved with many and frequent *tuak* toasts. It is considered impolite to refuse the first drink and caution needs to be exercised by novices on subsequent toasts.

Different variations of the harvest festival are celebrated throughout Borneo with those communities closer to Christianity being more pious, placing greater emphasis on prayers and much less on *tuak* toasts.

Hari Raya Puasa (Eid al-Fitr in Kalimantan)

This festival falls at the end of the Muslim fasting month of Ramadan, with the actual day determined by the sighting of a new moon by religious leaders. During Ramadan Muslims abstain from food and drink from the break of dawn until sunset to cleanse their souls and remind them of the sufferings of others who are less fortunate. Unlike much of the Muslim world, Borneo still operates during the day throughout Ramadan. It is possible to eat, but understandably the mood is quiet in the daytime. During the festivities that follow, many houses are gaily lit and decorated. Visits to a mosque for special prayers and later to homes of relatives are common in 'open houses', where family, friends and visitors are invited to share in the festivities.

Chinese New Year

Usually celebrated in late January or early February, this day marks the beginning of the Chinese lunar year. Traditionally on this day, parents present their children with small amounts of money wrapped in an *ang pow* (red packet) as a symbol of luck and good health. Friends and family are usually visited on the first and second days of the festivities.

Wesak Day (also spelt Vesak)

Marking the birth, enlightenment and death of Lord Buddha, this day is the most significant one in the Buddhist calendar. On this day Buddhist temples are full of worshippers and priests.

The Chinese believe that on the seventh moon of the lunar calendar, the Gates of Purgatory are opened and the souls of the dead are released from incarceration to mingle with humans for 30 days. To appease the neglected souls, the Chinese make offerings of food and candles. Incense is lit in rows, and sumptuous food offerings are made to pacify the ghosts. In most places Chinese operas are staged in various streets for all to enjoy.

Christmas Day, Good Friday

December 25 marks the birth of Christ and is celebrated in the spirit of good will with the call of peace and fellowship. The festive mood during the month of December culminates on Christmas Eve (December 24). Good Friday (the Friday before Easter Sunday) is also celebrated, especially by Ibans, who are mostly devout Christians and follow the Christian faith strictly. Good Friday is a state public holiday in both Sabah and Sarawak but a holiday is not granted in other parts of Malaysia.

Customs and Etiquette

Being a good guest is part of the travel experience and knowledge of the many customs helps to avoid embarrassment.

Responsible Tourism Guidelines

Tourism impacts upon the environment and the people living in that environment. Travellers who are concerned about such negative influences should consider their own personal impacts and adopt more sustainable practices in their travels. Everyone can make a difference in their own small way. Here are a few practical ideas that should assist in reducing the negative impacts of tourism.

• Support local businesses as an incentive for them to preserve natural habitats. While haggling over prices in markets may be fun, it is not universally practised especially in remote areas where prices maybe high due to extra transportation costs.

• Do not harm, destroy or remove plants or animals from their natural setting.

• Do not buy products made from threatened natural resources including shells and turtle products.

• Stick to jungle tracks to minimise erosion, plant destruction and most importantly; getting lost.

• Be wary around native animals; even the Orangutan rehabilitation centres are not zoos; these are wild animals, that can do wild things. Keep a safe distance and follow the instructions of guides who are familiar with the behaviour of these creatures.

• Waste disposal is a problem in many places especially islands and remote areas – remove unnecessary packaging before travelling to remote areas and recycle it where possible. Failing that; take it out with you and dispose of it appropriately. While some recycling occurs, it is not commonly practised throughout most of Borneo.

• Travel with biodegradable soaps and washing powers and use them sparingly.

• Buy a refillable water flask, carry it with you always and avoid buying water in plastic bottles ('refill rather than landfill').

• Ask or indicate to people prior to taking photographs as many local villagers do not like being photographed (do not photograph people bathing or washing).

• There are many religious and cultural sensitivities that travellers need to be aware of and asking guides or village headman is the best way to avoid offending the locals.

• Some areas around longhouses are religious sites although this may not be apparent – ask the villagers and they will be happy to explain their culture and discuss any activities that are taboo.

• Some communities do not encourage alcoholic or even cigarette consumption – ask so as to avoid offending anyone.

Customs

Different communities follow different customs, but here are a few generalizations to help smooth the path of travel.

- Many locals remove their shoes before entering buildings, especially homes and places of worship; visitors are expected to do the same.
- Muslims use the right hand only when eating, and eating with the hand is not uncommon.
- Many women do not shake hands with men so it is best to wait until a hand is offered.
- Many sections of mosques are not open to non-Muslims and it is best to

avoid mosques during prayers.
- Alcohol is not freely available, especially in Brunei, where it is not sold at all. Some Christian communities in Sarawak are also alcohol free.
- Placing the locals in a situation where they lose face should be avoided.
- Visitors should be aware of what *halal* and *haram* mean. *Halal* food refers to meat slaughtered according to Muslim law, and no pork or alcohol. *Haram* refers to non-Muslim items such as pork and alcohol
- In remote areas, tourists are rarely seen and the locals are curious. This extra interest may frustrate some but is usually harmless.
- The people of Borneo are modest in their dress and expect visitors to show constraint – nude bathing is out, as is revealing clothing, and public displays of affection are frowned upon. Respectable clothing is best worn when visiting government offices.
- Formal attire is interpreted variously in different parts of Borneo. Tourists who are invited to a function should enquire of their host what attire is expected. For men, a long-sleeved *batik* shirt is the height of formality in some circles. Dress codes are often enforced in some evening venues but smart casual wear is usually enough to open doors.
- During the fasting month of Ramadan, which varies from year to year, Muslims fast from sunrise to sunset, and it is respectful to avoid eating or drinking in front of them. Food and drinks are difficult to obtain during the day in many restaurants while Ramadan is observed.
- Drinking rice wine, or *tuak*, is a tradition in many tribal longhouses, and it is expected that visitors join in. It has a kick and caution is advised.
- Bargaining or haggling over prices is often part of the retail banter on Borneo especially for some items in some markets. However, it is not a universal practice and never part of shopping in department stores. Shoppers have to make up their own mind as to how much they want an item and how much a few sen here and there mean to them. Remember, this is the livelihood of the locals and not a tourist game so be prepared for a blunt refusal if you bargain too hard.
- Using and importing drugs is a capital offence in all of Borneo.

Tourist Assistance

Before travel, research embassy or consulate contact details in case it becomes necessary to get in touch with them. The same can be said for toll-free numbers for any travel insurance taken out. Tourist police are on hand to assist in Malaysia.

Staying in Touch

These days nearly everyone is connected to the world via a smartphone or the Internet. All but the remotest villages are accessible to a phone or Internet provider. Local SIM cards are available on arrival at major airports, and the Internet is freely available in most hotels. Cable television with international news is also available.

Electricity in Borneo is powered by 220–240 V, with some villages dependent on generators or solar power. Bario in Sarawak's remote east is powered by a solar hybrid power station as an initiative of Sarawak Energy.

Sarawak, Sabah and Brunei are one hour ahead of Kalimantan.

Getting There and Travelling

Many parts of Borneo are not easy to access, especially the rugged and often forested interior. Small planes, helicopters, rivers and four-wheel drive logging roads provide limited access, and in many cases long journeys need to be undertaken.

By Air

Airlines based in Malaysia, such as Malaysia Airlines, AirAsia, MASwings and Malindo (reportedly to change its name to Batik Air), fly to various destinations in Borneo. MASwings is a division of Malaysia Airlines that mostly services routes in Sarawak and Sabah, including remote destinations with small airstrips. It also flies internationally to Pontianak, Tarakan and Bandar Seri Begawan.

SilkAir flies from Singapore to Kuching and Kota Kinabalu, while Singapore Airlines flies to Bandar Seri Begawan. The Bruneian capital possibly has the best international connections on Royal Brunei Airlines to various regional and long-hail destinations including London, Melbourne, Dubai, Shanghai, Kuala Lumpur and Singapore as well as several destinations in Brunei itself.

Kuala Lumpur is the international gateway for many people travelling to Sarawak and Sabah, although there are some direct international flights to Kota Kinabalu from China, the Philippines, Korea, Australia and Brunei.

A number of Indonesian airlines, such as Garuda Indonesia, Lion, Malindo and Sriwijaya, fly to various destinations in Borneo.

Small airstrips in remote destinations (many destinations starting with 'Long') are serviced by small aircraft, typically Twin Otters. In others, helicopters provide the only air access. Luggage is limited on these flights, and travellers on an extended holiday in Borneo may have to store luggage at larger airports before flying in and out of these small destinations.

By Train

The railway from Kota Kinabalu to Tenom in Sabah is the only passenger railway in Borneo. Two trains use sections of the line, with the North Borneo Railway tourist steam train operating on Wednesdays and Saturdays from Tanjung Aru (Kota Kinabalu) south to Papar. Sabah State Railway operates services to Beaufort, and a few per day through to the inland town of Tenom.

There are ambitious plans to develop railways in Kalimantan, but these will mostly be to transport minerals from inland mines to coastal ports.

By Ferry

Ferries link Borneo to other destinations in the region as well as within Borneo. Because they are cheaper than flights, ferries are popular with the locals. Some popular routes are Kota Kinabalu to Labuan, Bandar Seri Begawan to Labuan, and Tawau to Nunukan/Tarakan.

There are numerous inter-island connections between the many Indonesian islands, with most being operated by Pelni, from Jakarta, Semarang and Surabaya on the island of Java to various destinations in Borneo, including Pontianak, Ketapang, Kumai, Banjarmasin, Balikpapan and Tarakan.

By River

Numerous vessels ply the rivers of Borneo,

from large express boats to sleek wooden dugouts, and passengers sometimes have to get out to assist a boatman in negotiating shallow river sections. In some Kalimantan national parks, liveaboard boats are popular with those spending a few days there.

By Road

Road travel (car, long-distance taxi, van, bus or bike) along roads of varying quality is one of the main ways to get around in Borneo. The roads revert to trails in remote parts, and walks of several days' duration appeal to the most intrepid travellers.

The Pan (or Trans) Borneo Highway is an ambitious plan to basically circumnavigate the island with certain sections in Sarawak, Brunei and Sabah already completed. The highway is mostly dual carriageway except for around large cities and towns where it widens. Being one of the few means of transportation, the road carries many forms of vehicles from small to big and slow to fast, which means anyone using the road needs to be careful as driving conditions can change suddenly. Roadworks do not always have advanced warning as in many other countries, and road washaways and landslides are not uncommon after heavy rain especially in steep mountainous areas. Cars often just stop on the road to unload goods or pick up people and those that break down may remain on the road rather than the shoulder for longer than they should (a snapped-off branch stuck at the rear of the vehicle will indicate to other motorists, may be all too late, that it is immobile). The message is to drive as if anything may happen, as sure enough, it probably will.

Long-distance buses and mini-vans are cheap means of traversing Borneo and most big towns have a bus depot on the outskirts where passengers board buses or air-conditioned, long-distance coaches.

Mini vans operate to the suburbs in large cities and towns, and connect to the more remote parts of the island. As they are often the only means many locals have to access the outside world, they have many uses from transporting people to accommodating produce destined for the market, such as fruit, vegetables and often small live animals. As such, they often get crowded and overloaded and do not provide the most comfortable form of transportation.

Hitchhiking is not a common practice but in remote parts of Borneo, people with a vehicle are usually helpful and open to offering a lift either for free or some small change. In some instances, long-distance buses drop passengers on main roads and may not go the extra few kilometres down the side road to the tourist attraction that is so appealing to foreign tourists. A good example is the side road leading to Sepilok Orangutan Rehabilitation Centre outside of Sandakan that is 2km (1.25 miles) from the main Sandakan-Ranau Road and visitors using public transport may find they have to alight here. The locals can identify a lost tourist from a distance and looking helpless and in need of a lift may save a longer than expected walk. Enterprising taxi drivers or motorcyclists often wait at these junctions to provide a lift for a fee.

In other areas, the only form of transportation is on the back of a motorcycle and passengers doing so shouldn't expect protection such as a motorcycle helmet.

Resources

Books

Bowden, D. 2012. *Enchanting Malaysia.* John Beaufoy Publishing.
Bowden, D. 2015. *Enchanting Indonesia.* John Beaufoy Publishing.
Bowden, D. 2016. *Enchanting Borneo.* John Beaufoy Publishing.
Das, I. 2012. *A Naturalist's Guide to the Snakes of Southeast Asia.* John Beaufoy Publishing.
Davison, G. W. H. & Aik, Y. C. 2010. *A Naturalist's Guide to the Birds of Malaysia.* John Beaufoy Publishing.
Davison, G., Payne, J. & M. Gumal. 2014. *Wild Malaysia.* John Beaufoy Publishing.
Guan, S. L. 2019 *A Naturalist's Guide to the Trees of Southeast Asia.* John Beaufoy Publishing.
Hutton, W. & Prudente, C. 2014, *Tabin – Sabah's Greatest Wildlife Sanctuary.* Tabin Wildlife Resort.
Janssen, J. & Sy, E. 2019. *A Naturalist's Guide to the Lizards of Southeast Asia.* John Beaufoy Publishing.
Kassem, K. & E. Madeja. 2014. *The Coral Triangle.* John Beaufoy Publishing.
Phillipps, Q. & K. Phillipps. 2014. *Phillipps' Field Guide to the Birds of Borneo.* John Beaufoy Publishing.
Phillipps, Q. & K. Phillipps. 2016. *Phillipps' Field Guide to the Mammals of Borneo and Their Ecology.* John Beaufoy Publishing.
Shepherd, C. R. & Shepherd, L.A. 2012. *A Naturalist's Guide to the Mammals of Southeast Asia.* John Beaufoy Publishing.
Shepherd, C. R. & Shepherd, L.A. 2017. *A Naturalist's Guide to the Primates of Southeast Asia.* John Beaufoy Publishing.
Silver, Lynette Ramsay. 2000. *Conspiracy of Silence,* Synergy Books International.
Wallace, A. R. 2016. *The Malay Archipelago.* John Beaufoy Publishing.
Wong, T.S. 2018. *A Naturalist's Guide to the Birds of Borneo.* John Beaufoy Publishing.
Yong, D. L. & Low, B. W. 2018. *The 125 Best Birdwatching Sites in Southeast Asia.* John Beaufoy Publishing.

Websites

Borneo Jazz Festival: www.borneojazz.com
Brunei Tourism: www.tourismbrunei.com
Heart of Borneo: www.heartofborneo.org
North Borneo Railway: www.northborneorailway.com.my
North Borneo Safari: www.northborneosafari.com
Orangutan Foundation International: www.orangutan.org
Rainforest World Music Festival: www.rwmf.net
Sabah Parks: www.sabahparks.org.my
Sabah State Railway: www.railway.sabah.gov.my
Sabah Tourism: www.sabahtourism.com
Sabah Wildlife Department: www.wildlife.sabah.gov.my
Sarawak Forestry: www.forestry.sarawak.gov.my
Sarawak Museum: www.museum.sarawak.gov.my
Sarawak Cultural Village: www.scv.com.my
Sarawak Tourism: sarawaktourism.com
Tabin Wildlife Resort: www.tabinwildlife.com.my
The Orangutan Project: www.orangutan.org.au
World Land Trust: www.worldlandtrust.org
World Wide Fund for Nature: www.worldwildlife.org

Travel Specialists

Malaysia
Asian Overland Services (www.asianoverland.com.my). They also have offices in Kota Kinabalu (+60 88 212-170) and Kuching (+60 82 330-398).
Asian Trails (www.asiantrails.travel).
Diethelm Travel (www.diethelmtravel.com). They also have offices in Kota Kinabalu (+60 88 266-353) and Kuching (+60 82 412-778).

Sabah
Bike Borneo (www.bikeborneo.com) are based in Kota Kinabalu and organize tailor-made bicycle tours and other adventure activities in Borneo, especially Sabah.
Borneo Escapade Tours (www.borneoescpade.com).
Borneo Eco Tour (www.borneoecotours.com). They have offices in Kota Kinabalu (+60 88 438-300), Sandakan (+60 89 663-210) and Sukau (+60 13 811-4019).
Borneo Nature Tours (www.borneonature.tours.com) is the operator of Borneo Rainforest Lodge in Danum Valley.
North Borneo Safari (www.cedeprudente.com), operated by acclaimed photographer and respected travel professional.
Sticky Rice Travel (www.stickyrice.com), boutique, niche travel company practicing responsible tourism and cultural immersion plus customized tours in Sabah and Sarawak.

Sarawak
Borneo Adventure (www.borneoadventure.com)
Borneo Exploration Tour & Travel (www.borneoexplorers.com.my).
Greatown Travel (www.greatown.com) – Sibu area travel specialists.
Minda Nusantara Tours and Travel Agencies (www.mindatravel.com) are a Miri-based travel company.

Brunei
Ulu Ulu Resort (www.uluuluresort.com) have entered into a public-private partnership with the Government of Brunei to operate a resort and tours in Brunei's only national park, Ulu Temburong.

Indonesian Kalimantan
Adventure Indonesia (www.adventureindonesia.tours) offer customized tours and have offices in Jakarta and Central Kalimantan.
Musi Holidays (www.musiholidays.co.id).
Seven World Tours (www.sevenworldtours.com).
Tari Travel (www.taritravelindonesia.com).

Australia
Borneo Ethical Adventure (www.borneoethical.com), small group and responsible travel specialists.
Borneo Tour Specialists (www.borneo.com.au).
Intrepid Travel (www.intrepidtravel.com).
Peregrine Adventures (www.peregrineadventures.com).
Wendy Wu Tours (www.wendywutours.com.au).

Germany
G Adventures (www.gadventures.com).

United Kingdom
Abercrombie & Kent (www.abercrombiekent.co.uk).
Exodus Travel (www.exodus.co.uk). Exodus also have offices in various overseas destinations including Australia, Ireland, Netherlands, New Zealand, South Africa and the USA.

Hayes & Jarvis (www.hayesandjarvis.co.uk).
Reef and Rainforest
(www.reefandrainforest.co.uk).
Responsible Travel
(www.responsibletravel.com).

United States
Borneo Travel & Tours (www.borneousa.com).

Some Basic Bahasa Phrases

thank you	*terimah kasih*
you're welcome	*sama sama*
welcome	*selamat datang*
my name is	*nama saya*
good morning	*selamat pagi*
good afternoon	*selamat petang*
good evening	*selamat malam*
where is ..?	*dimana*
how much is this ..?	*ini berapa*
one	*satu*
two	*dua*
three	*tiga*
100	*se ratus*
1,000	*se ribu*
bus station	*setsen bus*
taxi	*teksi*
beach	*pantai*
island	*pulau*
hill	*bukit*
mountain	*gunung*
river	*sungai*
town	*bandar*
water	*air*
eat	*makan*
drink	*minum*
expensive	*mahal*
cheap	*murah*
can	*boleh*
cannot	*tak boleh*
man	*lelaki*
woman	*perempuan*
toilet	*tandas*

ACKNOWLEDGEMENTS

While many people contributed to this book, specific thanks are extended to Hestin Klass, Dony Prayudi, Mohammad Shafie Obet, Jerudong Park Playground, Kevin Nila Nangai, Rory Richardson and Ken Scriven.

Photo Credits

All photos taken by David Bowden except for the following:
Borneo Rainforest Lodge 80, 82; Brunei Tourism 122, 126, 129; Erik Fearn 124; Indonesian Ministry of Tourism 132, 134/135, 136, 144; Jerudong Park 128; Malaysia Tourism 84, 85; Dony Prayudi 140, 141, 142; Sabah Tourism 46, 48, 50; Sarawak Tourism 108, 114; Shutterstock/Andreas H 138; Silk Air 130; Wong Tsu Shi 24, 25 (top)

Index